A 1568 Portuguese map by Vaz Dourado of the southern tip of South America.

COVER: *Detail from* The Debarkation of Christopher Columbus, *by Edward Moran.*

FRONT ENDSHEET: *Magellan's world voyage traced on a map made around 1545.*

BACK ENDSHEET: *Sir Francis Drake's fleet in harbor at Santo Domingo, 1585.*

THE AMERICAN HERITAGE
NEW ILLUSTRATED HISTORY
OF THE UNITED STATES

VOLUME 1

THE NEW WORLD

By ROBERT G. ATHEARN
Professor of History, University of Colorado

CREATED AND DESIGNED BY THE EDITORS OF
AMERICAN HERITAGE
The Magazine of History

PUBLISHED BY
DELL PUBLISHING CO., INC., NEW YORK

CONTENTS OF THE COMPLETE SERIES

Foreword by JOHN F. KENNEDY
Introduction by ALLAN NEVINS
Main text by ROBERT G. ATHEARN

A MASTER INDEX FOR ALL 16 VOLUMES APPEARS IN VOLUME 16

NETHERLANDS

SPAIN

ENGLAND

PORTUGAL

FRANCE

CONTENTS OF VOLUME 1

FOREWORD

JOHN F. KENNEDY

1917 – 1963

There is little that is more important for an American citizen to know than the history and traditions of his country. Without such knowledge, he stands uncertain and defenseless before the world, knowing neither where he has come from nor where he is going. With such knowledge, he is no longer alone but draws a strength far greater than his own from the cumulative experience of the past and a cumulative vision of the future.

Knowledge of our history is, first of all, a pleasure for its own sake. The American past is a record of stirring achievement in the face of stubborn difficulty. It is a record filled with figures larger than life, with high drama and hard decision, with valor and with tragedy, with incidents both poignant and picturesque, and with the excitement and hope involved in the conquest of a wilderness and the settlement of a continent. For the true historian—and for the true student of history— history is an end in itself. It fulfills a deep human need for understanding, and the satisfaction it provides requires no further justification.

Yet, though no further justification is required for the study of history, it would not be correct to say that history serves no further use than the satisfaction of the historian. History, after all, is the memory of a nation. Just as memory enables the individual to learn, to choose goals and stick to them, to avoid making the same mistake twice—in short, to grow—so history is the means by which a nation establishes its sense of identity and purpose. The future arises out of the past, and a country's history is a statement of the values and hopes which, having forged what has gone before, will now forecast what is to come.

As a means of knowledge, history becomes a means of judgment. It offers an understanding of both the variety and unity of a nation whose credo is *E Pluribus Unum*—out of many, one. It reminds us of the diverse abundance of our people, coming from all races and all parts of the world, of our fields and mountain ranges, deserts and great rivers, our green farmlands and the thousand voices of our cities. No revolution in communication or transportation can destroy the fact that this continent is, as Walt Whitman said, "a nation of nations." Yet it also reminds us that, in spite of the diversity of ethnic origin, of geographic locale, of occupation, of social status, of religious creed, of political commitment, Americans are united by an ancient and encompassing faith in progress, justice, and freedom.

Our history thus tests our policy: Our past judges our present. Of all the disciplines, the study of the folly and achievements of man is best calculated to foster the critical sense of what is permanent and meaningful amid the mass of superficial and transient questions which make up the day-to-day clamor. The history of our nation tells us that every action taken *against* the freedoms of conscience and expression, *against* equality before the law and equality of opportunity, *against* the ordinary men and women of the country is an action taken *against* the American tradition. And it tells us that every action taken *for* a larger freedom and a more equal and spacious society is one more step toward the realization of what Herbert Croly once called "the promise of American life."

A knowledge of history is more than a means of judgment: It is also a means of sympathy—a means of relating our own experience with the experience of other peoples and lands struggling for national fulfillment. We may sometimes forget, for example, that the United States began as an underdeveloped nation which seized its independence by carrying out a successful revolution against a colonial empire. We may forget that, in the first years of the new republic, George Washington laid down the principle of no "permanent alliances" and enjoined the United States to a course of neutralism in the face of the great-power conflicts then dividing the civilized world. We may forget that, in the first stages of our economic development, our national growth was stimulated to a considerable degree by "foreign aid"—that is, investment from abroad—and by public investment and direction on the part of our state and local as well as our national government. We may forget that our own process of economic change was often accompanied by the issue of wildcat paper money, by the repudiation of bonds, by disorder, fraud, and violence. If we recall the facts of our own past, we may better understand the problems and predicaments of contemporary "new nations" laboring for national development in circumstances far less favorable than our own—and we will, in consequence, become less liable to the national self-righteousness which is both unworthy of our own traditions and a bane of international relations.

A knowledge of history is, in addition, a means of strength. "In times of change and danger," John Dos Passos wrote just before World War II, "when there is a quicksand of fear under men's reasoning, a sense of continuity with generations gone before can stretch like a life line across the scary present." Dos Passos called his book *The Ground We Stand On*—and the title concisely defines the role of the past in preparing us for the crisis of the present and the challenge of the future. When Americans fight for individual liberty, they have Thomas Jefferson and James Madison beside them; when they strive for social justice, they strive alongside Andrew Jackson and Franklin Roosevelt; when they work for peace and a world community, they work with Woodrow Wilson; when they fight and die in wars to make men free, they fight and die with Abraham Lincoln. Historic continuity with the past, as Justice Oliver Wendell Holmes said, "is not a duty; it is only a necessity."

A knowledge of history is, above all, a means of responsibility—of responsibility to the past and of responsibility to the future . . . of responsibility to those who came before us and struggled and sacrificed to pass on to us our precious inheritance of freedom . . . and of responsibility to those who will come after us and to whom we must pass on that inheritance with what new strength and substance it is within our power to add. "Fellow citizens," Abraham Lincoln said, "we cannot escape history. . . . The fiery trial through which we pass will light us down, in honor or dishonor, to the latest generation." American history is not something dead and over. It is always alive, always growing, always unfinished—and every American today has his own contribution to make to the great fabric of tradition and hope which binds all Americans, dead and living and yet to be born, in a common faith and a common destiny.

INTRODUCTION

ALLAN NEVINS

How are we to approach our American history? It is, first of all, a throbbing, human, vital story—dramatic and colorful. Any author who makes it fascinating, without falsifying it, is probably telling it well.

Every generation has to rewrite its history. But each new version has to have a pattern, a design, and within limits each of us has a right to say what it should be.

The most usual pattern has been to make our past a grand success story. That was the approach which George Bancroft used a century ago and which others have followed. The voice of our best American commentators has nearly always been an optimistic voice, and foreign observers have struck the same note of optimism. All describe achievement after achievement—the raw continent settled, independence gained, an efficient government established, the scope of democracy widened, national unity confirmed in the Civil War, slavery abolished, poverty increasingly reduced, opportunity thrown open to all, two perilous world wars won, and the leadership of free peoples gallantly assumed.

This approach to American history seems the more convincing because our record over the past two centuries does contrast happily with that of less fortunate lands. But if we look carefully at the seamy side of the record and weigh the irrational, blundering, wasteful, and corrupt conduct of large groups and their leaders, we may well have doubts. The tendency of Americans simply to *drift* when strenuous and well-planned action

was needed has often been especially distressing. Ours *is* a success story, but it is not that alone.

Another approach to our past has seen it as the story of an expanding democracy. Much can be said for this concept, which brings the plain people into the center of the picture. It has the seal of high authority. The distinctive trait of our republic, said Abraham Lincoln, is that it was "conceived in liberty and dedicated to the proposition that all men are created equal"—that is, it was by the principles of its origin democratic. Europeans have always regarded the United States as the world's major experiment in democracy.

But democracy is an ideal at once simple and complex. It has to be broken down into three distinct parts: *Political democracy,* which we have gained and kept only by constant fighting; *social democracy,* of which we have had more than most nations, but which has not prevented the emergence in every generation of class lines; and *economic democracy,* of which we have had little for long periods.

History shows that these three parts of democracy are often in partial conflict. For example, our lack of economic democracy between 1870 and 1910, when colossal fortunes stood beside abysmal poverty, gravely crippled our political and our social democracy.

If both the success-story and the expanding-democracy analysis of our history are inadequate and even misleading, what then? James Truslow Adams declared that the true key to an understanding of our past is to be found in the search for the "American dream." The Europeans who came in successive waves believed that they could hew out a better destiny, that they could find more security, more freedom, more scope for their talents, more happiness—in short, a richer, nobler life. Sometimes the American dream failed, as in the terrible tragedy of the Civil War and its deplorable aftermath; never has it been perfectly realized. Moreover, it has varied from section to section—the Southern planter's dream of 1850 was totally different from that of the Northern farmer; from group to group—the dream of the frontiersman was quite unlike that of the immigrant in the New York sweatshop; from era to era—a crowded industrial nation of 190,000,000 can make but limited use of the Jeffersonian dream, so well adapted to our youthful agrarian republic. Yet the American dream remains a guiding light and has value for interpreting our history.

What we have in common is a *national character*. So we believe, and so the whole world believes. It changes from generation to generation, from century to century. Assuredly it is less individualistic than it was in the days of the Founding Fathers, but it is more disciplined, more social-minded, more world-conscious. Can anyone doubt that our faith in ourselves and our destiny is any less fervent? There is evidence that it has even deepened. We are far wealthier now; we have witnessed an explosion of population, of affluence, of leisure. But has not our idealism kept pace with our material advance?

When Sir Ernest Barker wrote his *National Character and the Factors in Its Formation* a generation ago, he divided the formative factors into two groups—material and spiritual. He listed the chief material factors as racial (genetic), geographical, and economic. He gave them only a third of his book. The spiritual factors are much more numerous. They include law, governmental institutions, religion, language, literature, thought, and education. To *them* he gave fully two-thirds, indicating that he believed the greatest forces in history to have been the spiritual ones. What single element, he asks at one point, stands out above all others in shaping English civilization? His answer is the Common Law of England—the only great system of jurisprudence in the world besides the Roman. Barker believes it has had a deeper influence on the temper and behavior of the British people than any other single force.

What has been the paramount factor in shaping the American character? Has it been our special conception of individual liberty? Undoubtedly it has been a spiritual and not a material force, but which one? In these volumes diligent seekers may well find the answer.

Readers of this work may be repaid in many ways for the time and attention they give to it. The *main text* objectively presents the basic facts of American history, with enough interpretation to stimulate further pondering over means and ends, causes and effects. The *special picture portfolios* give to personalities and events a depth and vividness that too often elude words alone. And the *special contribution*—an article at the end of each volume—gives a close-up on a subject treated more generally elsewhere.

All in all, readers will find here a story varied in human interest, dramatic in impact, and at times inspiring—illustrated by drawings, paintings, and photographs, many by eyewitnesses or contemporaries, of a variety and quality never before offered in such a work. Readers will also find food for imagination—events and achievements that can stir the mind as few novelists can ever stir it, because what *happened* far transcends any make-believe.

9

CHAPTER 1

EUROPE MOVES WEST

Before dawn on October 12, 1492, three small vessels under the command of a Genoese sailor named Christopher Columbus pushed their way westward near a tiny island in the Bahamas. Suddenly Rodrigo de Triana, a lookout on the *Pinta,* sighted a shadowy form dead ahead. It was too massive to be a floating object. With the cry *"Tierra! Tierra!"* he brought the ship awake, and quickly its captain signaled Columbus of the discovery. "You *did* find land!" Columbus shouted to him. "I give you 5,000 maravedis as a bonus." With sails shortened, the *Santa María, Pinta,* and *Niña* hove to, their crews waiting impatiently for sunrise.

Daylight brought a view of the first land seen in the Western Hemisphere by any Europeans, save perhaps the earlier Norsemen. On the western side of the island the seamen found a protected bay and, as the startled natives ashore looked on, a small boat bearing the royal standard of Spain was landed. After kneeling on the sand

Columbus plants the Cross in the New World, thus opens the great period of exploration of the Americas. From a 1665 fresco.

and thanking God for a safe voyage, Columbus arose and named the bit of land San Salvador. Relations were then begun with the natives, whom the newcomers called Indians. Red caps, glass beads, and other articles of small value were bartered for skeins of cotton thread, parrots, and darts. European contact with the American native would continue for nearly 400 years, until he was traded out of almost all his land and belongings.

After a day or so of rest, the explorer took his ships deeper into the Caribbean, sighting Cuba, which he explained to his men was Japan. In December they discovered Hispaniola and there put up a small fort, garrisoning it with a handful of men. By March of 1493, Columbus landed at Lisbon and announced to the world that he had seen the Indies. The Portuguese were both excited and dubious. Here was a man who had accomplished by sailing westward what they had taken a century to do by rounding the Cape of Good Hope.

What caused Columbus to make a journey of such length and danger? Did it mean that Europe was overcrowded, fully exploited economically, shorn of all its opportunities? Or was this simply a breed of man endowed with an overdeveloped sense of adventure? The answer perhaps lies in Spain's eagerness to keep abreast of the Portuguese, now Europe's most renowned navigators, and to participate in the greatest expansion the Christian world had yet experienced.

During Columbus' century—the 15th—Europe began to emerge from its old local isolations. The feudal system, tied to the local authority of minor warlords, was beginning to give way to the modern national state, a more powerful and permanent political organization. As the authority of the feudal lords dwindled, many of those who had lived under them moved toward the cities. Europe, still predominantly agricultural, was now going in a direction that took men away from a mere subsistence economy, where they raised most of their necessities on a small plot of ground, to a money, or profit, economy. As the artisan class began to grow, and articles for sale were produced in larger quantities, the enterprising merchant (the traveling salesman of his time) began to move out in an ever-widening circle from his home town. Local trade routes, little used for hundreds of years, now saw a growing traffic, and peddlers passing through told fascinating tales of other areas. This resulted in a curiosity to know more about lands farther away. The increased travel and trade meant that the methods of transpor-

Marco Polo is seen setting out fro
24 years later, and his report of t

*...ice in 1271 on his journey to China. He returned
...new world in the East intrigued the Europeans.*

tation, particularly by water, were soon to be expanded and improved. It also meant the rise of the city.

The rise of the city was extremely important to later explorations. Although by 1500 only one-tenth of Europe's population was urban, the growing towns were strategically located from the standpoint of commerce. London, Hamburg, Antwerp, and Lisbon were built near the mouths of rivers, while Paris, Mainz, and Ghent stood close to river junctions. By today's standards these places were small. When Columbus sailed for America, London had only 50,000 people. Constantinople, Europe's largest city, had 250,000; Paris, 200,000; Ghent, 135,000. But they were populous and important for their time, and the association with water transportation destined them to be the metropolitan areas of the future. It can be questioned whether, without such places, we would have had universities, great inventions, or a flourishing art—or, for that matter, whether Columbus would have made his great find. As centers of trade, Europe's cities now became not only powerful independent bastions, but springboards for further economic venture.

If Europe at this time was broken into small political segments, it still had a religious unity. The Catholic Church was dominant and all-powerful. Yet the Church served as a stimulant rather than a deterrent to most businesses and to commerce. For example, its crusading fervor took men to all parts of the known world in search of converts, and as they moved around, they could not help noticing new and different articles that would be useful in trade. Even the monastic orders were producers of such salable goods as wine, grain, and cloth. Finally, extensive travel back and forth from all Europe to the Continent's religious capital, Rome, served to broaden men's knowledge of opportunities throughout the land.

The Crusades, which during the 12th and 13th centuries attempted to free the Holy Land from non-Christians, stirred Europe considerably. In some cases the great movement amounted to a nationwide effort as kings were persuaded to employ large forces in the Middle East. The overall result was that thousands of individuals, from baronial knights down to propertyless workers, traveled farther away from home than they ever had before. Eastward, beyond the Mediterranean, they encountered a strange new civilization, rich beyond belief. Spices, silks, and other luxury items excited their imaginations, and if they could not all bring home samples of

The merchants in this 1497 miniature were part of the Hanseatic League, a mercantile association of German towns. Business is discussed in the city of Hamburg, while the ships lying in the harbor prepare to carry metalware, silks, and linens from the cities of northern Europe to the seaports of the eastern Baltic.

Godfrey of Bouillon, leader of the first crusading army, prepares to sail to the East, as confident as William the Conqueror. In fact, his ship looked more like one of William's than does this fanciful, overcrowded 14th-century vessel.

their finds, they certainly carried back stories of all they had seen.

Transportation facilities developed rapidly, as always, when wars are fought at a distance. More soldiers had to be moved farther than ever before, and out of the need arose an important shipbuilding industry at such places of embarkation as the Italian cities. No sea captain likes to come home with an empty vessel, and be-

fore the religious wars were very old, large quantities of Eastern goods made their appearance in Europe. Livestock in Europe was small and rangy, all muscle and bone, and its meat was much more palatable after an application of such spices as pepper. Here was a type of merchandise that the seamen could bring back in quantity and sell at a high price. Then there were the nobles who were eager to have fine cloth and jewels with which to bedeck themselves and set themselves apart from the lesser nobles or even their own serfs. No enterprising businessmen could overlook this market. Out of the possibilities for sudden gain arose a powerful and active merchant class. These men were ingenious, ambitious, willing to take a risk, and always desirous of finding new sources of goods and new methods of bringing them to market. If they read of Marco Polo's travels, their determination to expand operations doubtless rose to new heights.

The Turks—unwelcome interlopers

But in 1453 a trade barrier appeared. The Turks captured Constantinople, at the crossroads of this new and rich trade route, and with the conquest of Cairo in 1517 they would complete their domination of the Near East. This did not mean the end of trade. It meant only that another middleman had been added to the string that already handed on the goods from faraway lands. The Europeans now would have to deal with the Turks, or find a new route that would cut out these hopeful associates. It was not any refusal on the part of the Turk to join the new gold rush that caused European Christians to seek other routes. By circumventing the interlopers, merchants simply could realize greater dividends from their ventures. If an all-water route to the East could be found, it would mean cheaper transportation, larger

profits, and the pleasant prospect of dealing the Turks out of a new and highly profitable game. The idea was inviting enough to make men take long chances.

The upsurge in commercial life had a good many ramifications. Men were eager to learn more about other parts of the world, and the resulting intellectual activity sparked a renaissance in European cultural life. Their curiosity stemmed from a desire to find additional sources of luxuries, better methods of transportation, and wider markets for distribution. The emphasis was on the material—personal acquisition and gain. In their desire for worldly fame and personal achievement, men turned to the Greek classics to see what secrets they would reveal. When they found suggestions that the world was round and perhaps the East might be reached by sailing westward, they were interested. The idea was appealing because their experimentations had produced more efficient means of navigation, making such a journey feasible. The compass and the astrolabe (an instrument used to determine latitude) now were rather widely used. Charts and maps were constantly being improved and expanded. By 1600, men were better equipped than ever to sail great distances from home. With the powerful commercial stimulus, their ventures became more and more bold. The age of discovery was at hand.

Expeditions to discover new trade routes could be organized in several

Prince Henry the Navigator

ways. The Italians learned early that the joint-stock company was one method. A number of men might join in a venture, sharing the risk and dividing the profits. The Crusades had shown that such an organization as the Church, combined with the resources of wealthy knights, could launch extensive projects. But it was the rise of the national state in Europe, whose various monarchs were avid for increased wealth and power, that saw most of the successful explorations completed. Prominent among these new nations was little Portugal, jutting westward into the Atlantic, and most strategically located for an important place in the coming world trade.

Portugal's young Prince Henry, who was to become known to the world as The Navigator, pushed one exploration after another southward along the African coast during the 15th century. He believed that when the huge land mass was passed, the way to fabled India would be clear. His conviction finally paid off. By 1488, Bartholomeu Diaz had rounded the Cape of Good Hope, and 10 years later Vasco da Gama reached India. When asked what had brought them so far, the sailors answered, "Christians and spices." Shortly the new trade route around Africa was in use, and the late Prince Henry's determination to develop it had caused a commercial revolution. Within a few years the Portuguese had plunged eastward all the way to China and Japan. No longer were the Italian cities the focal point in the Eastern trade. The center had shifted from the Mediterranean, now a mere lake, to the Atlantic, and the Iberian Peninsula soared to new importance.

Columbus puts Spain ahead

Because the rival Portuguese were so successful at exploration, the Spanish were willing to listen to the proposals of Columbus. Perhaps in more normal times his theory that the Indies could be reached more simply by sailing due west than by using the long and dangerous route around Africa might have been ignored. But the Spanish, whose rise to national power happened to coincide with the great period of maritime expansion, wanted some of the benefits of the new trade for themselves. After many doubts and delays, King Ferdinand and Queen Isabella gave Columbus the financial support necessary to carry out his geographical investigations. Sailing westward from Spain on August 3, 1492, he pushed his little fleet deep into the unknown Atlantic and raised a landfall by October 12. He was convinced that he had fulfilled his ambition to reach the Indies.

Although it soon developed that Columbus had found something other than the Indies in 1492, the Spanish continued to exploit and enlarge upon his discoveries. Columbus himself made three other voyages within the next few years, and before long Spain had embarked upon a colonial effort in the Americas that was not to end until 1898. Rival European nations were quick to see that the Admiral of the Ocean Sea had found something important, and soon their own ships headed west. As early as 1497 and 1498, John Cabot, flying British colors, ranged along the coast of present Canada and the United States. Giovanni da Verrazano, representing the French in 1524, coasted off the same shores. A generation before, in 1500, a Portuguese navigator named Pedro de Cabral claimed that he had touched a part of South America, and his sponsors soon hoisted their flag on what would be called Brazil. Meanwhile, Spanish ships penetrated western waters in larger numbers, expanding upon the original claims. Vasco de Balboa boldly crossed the Isthmus of Panama in 1513 and found still another ocean! A Florentine merchant named Amerigo Vespucci wrote so glowingly of one of these expeditions that a German geographer suggested

the newly opened part of the world be called America. Since it had been called everything from the Land of the Parrots to New India, to no one's satisfaction, the new and shorter name stuck. Columbus, who died impoverished, could not even will his name to the greatest discovery of the age.

After the initial disappointment at not having found the Indies wore off, the Spanish and all other Europeans realized that something of general interest had been uncovered. Men of the old continent, now on the verge of an economic boom, were deeply interested in enlarging their supply of

Giovanni da Verrazano

19

that well-known medium of exchange, gold. The prospect of finding additional products for exchange or manufacture also excited their appetites. The desire for personal wealth and the possibility of sudden financial ascendancy powered the drive of the Spanish in particular to exploit to the limit their new findings, and the Portuguese, fearful of losing out, complained about it. To settle any argument, the Pope drew a line down the map of the Atlantic in 1493, giving to Portugal eastern Brazil, Africa, the East Indies. Spain received most of America.

True, the new land did not yield up large troves of gems, bales of silks, or quantities of Oriental spices, but there were some returns to be had and they were not lost upon the explorers. As early as 1512, on the island of Hispaniola, where Columbus had founded the first colony in the Americas, the Spaniards were extracting a million dollars in gold annually. Aside from the mining, there were agricultural resources. Sugar cane, introduced into the West Indies by Columbus, promised to yield a profitable return. Equally important, places like Hispaniola provided a staging area for further explorations on the mainland, and it was from this vantage point that many a subsequent expedition was launched.

Newcomers to the Western Hemisphere found there groups of natives in varying stages of civilization. Columbus described the first ones he saw as being neither black nor white, but "the color of the Canary Islanders." The primitiveness of their culture was demonstrated to him when he handed them swords. Grasping the blades in ignorance, they cut themselves. They had seen their first iron. Concluding that the natives would make fine servants, and fit subjects for Christianizing, he took six home with him.

The aboriginal Americans

On the mainland there were larger groups of what the Spaniards called Indians. Such tribes as the Aztecs of Mexico and the Incas of Peru had a remarkably advanced political and economic organization. Instead of making the task of conquest harder, their civilization simplified it, for the Spanish, by controlling the leaders, easily subjugated the others. Later on, the English in North America would find the task of suppressing the wilder tribes a long and arduous one.

Each of the hundreds of tribes of American Indians had evolved its own culture in response to the demands and the resources of the environment in which it lived. The European was puzzled by the American Indian, and by his cultures, in which the complex and the primitive existed side by side. The Indian made beautiful baskets and pottery, skillfully decorated clothing of animal skins and fine cotton cloth, jewelry of shell and hammered silver and gold, elaborate houses and huge temples. Yet because he had never learned to make metal tools, he was limited to simple ones of stone, wood, bone, or shell. For transportation he had canoes, toboggans, and snowshoes, but he had never used the wheel.

To the sailors who had lived for weeks on ship's fare, the abundant food of the New World may have seemed more of a reward for crossing the ocean than the gold ingots and precious jewels. The Indians introduced the white man to strange and delicious edibles, many of which he promptly adopted. White potatoes and sweet potatoes, corn, squash, melons, pumpkins, kidney beans and Lima beans, chili peppers, avocados, pineapples, tomatoes, and peanuts went to Spain with the other spoils of the Americas.

The conquistador was the first white man to enjoy tobacco; to drink chocolate (from the cacao bean), the sacred drink of the Aztec Indians; to hear of the miracle cures wrought by quinine; and to taste vanilla. He saw the Indians playing a game with a resilient ball, which they made out of the milky sap of certain plants. This was Europe's introduction to rubber.

Obviously the American native was wholly unprepared for the arrival of the European. For centuries he had

In Peru, in 1532, the emperor of the Incas, Atahualpa, was carried on a golden throne to the camp of Pizarro, the Spanish explorer. When the emperor refused conversion to Christianity, the Spaniards began the slaughter depicted below.

enjoyed complete isolation and had not even suspected the existence of a place like Europe. During this time each of the native tribes had assumed control of a relatively small area of land and then settled down to rule it, knowing little of the adjacent country.

The Spanish especially had little difficulty in conquering South and Central America. The Indians were pleased to have European assistance in fighting their neighbors and welcomed the firearms, which gave them a vast superiority over their enemies, who knew nothing of such magic. Thus the Spanish did not have to divide and conquer. The natives were perfectly willing to fight one another, and before long the conquistadors, as the newcomers were called, controlled the land from Mexico to Patagonia. From then on it was a process of degradation for the Indian, either through enforced labor or the white man's vices and diseases, like liquor and smallpox. The same would be true of tribes in what is presently the United States, except that the process would be much slower.

The impact of America

The discovery by Columbus meant, in many ways, the rejuvenation of the Old World. In 1492, before the news of the rich new lands to the west brought visions of gold and adventure, the new century had been awaited with little hope. Medieval Europe, with its feudalism and its craft guilds, its monolithic Church and religion-dominated art and learning, was crumbling. The Church was being attacked on all sides. The fight against the infidel seemed hopeless; Constantinople had fallen to the Turks in 1453 and efforts to retrieve it for Christendom had failed. England and France had devoted the first half of the 15th century to fighting each other, the second half to trying to quash their powerful nobles. Spain as a nation had only just emerged out of loosely knit provinces. Except for the work of the Portuguese, there had been no significant breakthrough in geographic discovery for nearly a century.

Within a few years, however, the picture began to change. Stronger monarchs stamped out local opposition and proceeded determinedly on a course of nationalistic expansion. Now, with the Americas open and waiting for exploitation, the energies of Europe could be directed across the Atlantic. As an immediate revivifier, huge amounts of gold and silver began to flow through the economic arteries and the greatest boom Europe had ever known had started.

Now the westward rush was on. No respectable nation could be without its colony from which it could gain bullion and raw materials and in which it hoped to dispose of surplus manufactured materials. Like the eastern United States in later gold-rush days, Europe took full advantage of the virgin land to the west. For the next 400 years this was to be the story of America.

NEW YORK PUBLIC LIBRARY

THE SPANISH CONQUEST

"I discovered many islands inhabited by people without number; and I took possession of them all for Their Highnesses, by proclamation and hoisting the Royal Standard." Thus wrote Christopher Columbus to the court of Ferdinand and Isabella, reporting on one of history's most fateful voyages. He had touched and probed a New World of unimaginable riches and an unimaginable destiny, and he had stamped it with the seal of Spain. It was Spain that would find and seize and build upon the islands of the Caribbean, the fabulous kingdoms of Mexico and Central America, the rich fringes of the continent to the south and lands in the sea to the west. She would put down enduring roots in California and in what was to become the southwestern corner of the United States. With Spain more than with any other European nation, the opening of our hemisphere is identified. Her record of conquest in the New World was a patch-quilt of motives. Cruelty there was, and heroism; lust and sanctity; the desire to uplift and the greed to exploit. In the 1600 engraving (above), an Indian chief, angered by the quarreling of greedy conquistadors, contemptuously strikes down the tribute scales.

23

THE NIÑA'S PILOT MAKES A MAP

Juan de la Cosa, pilot-navigator of Columbus' *Niña,* drew the known world on oxhide in 1500. Cuba and nearby lands bear Spanish flags; the Americas are green—the color used for the unknown.

24

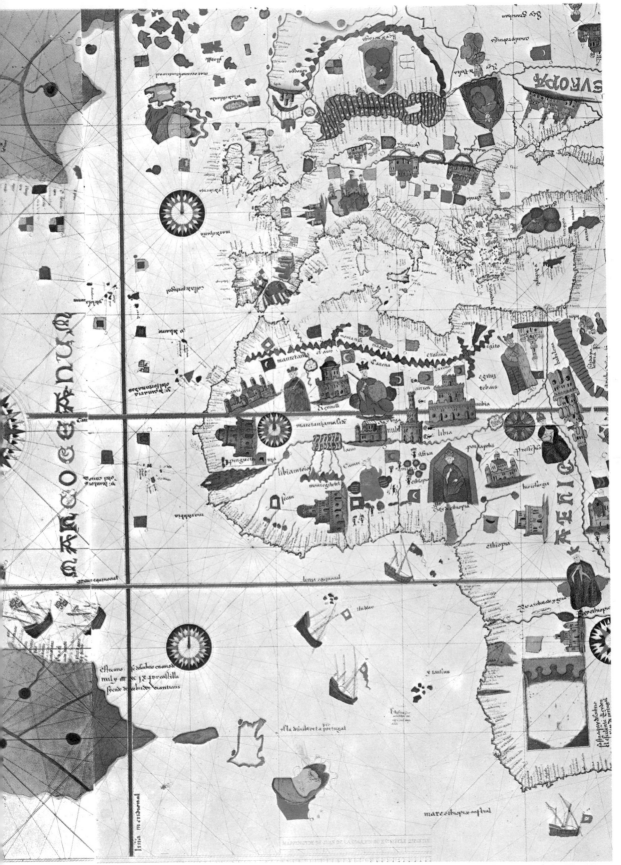

Left: Aztecs store food against famine—a real danger in drought-prone Mexico. Aztec slaves (right), often prisoners of war, sometimes sold their own children into bondage.

THE SPANISH CONQUEST

BEFORE THE SPANISH CAME

The conquistadors were often cruel and grasping, but the realities of Indian life itself—slavery, cannibalism, ruthless slaughter in war—were grim enough. On the opposite page is an Aztec tribute roll. Bordering glyphs at left and bottom represent conquered cities. Across the top are blankets of varying designs; the tree symbol meant 400 blankets of that type were to be paid. Below these are the other objects that were exacted as payment from the many subject peoples.

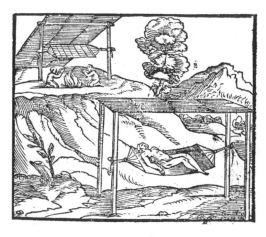

A contrast to the inventive Aztecs were the Caribs (left), cannibal fishermen of the islands. Primitive Venezuelans (right) invented the hammock; Spaniards soon copied it.

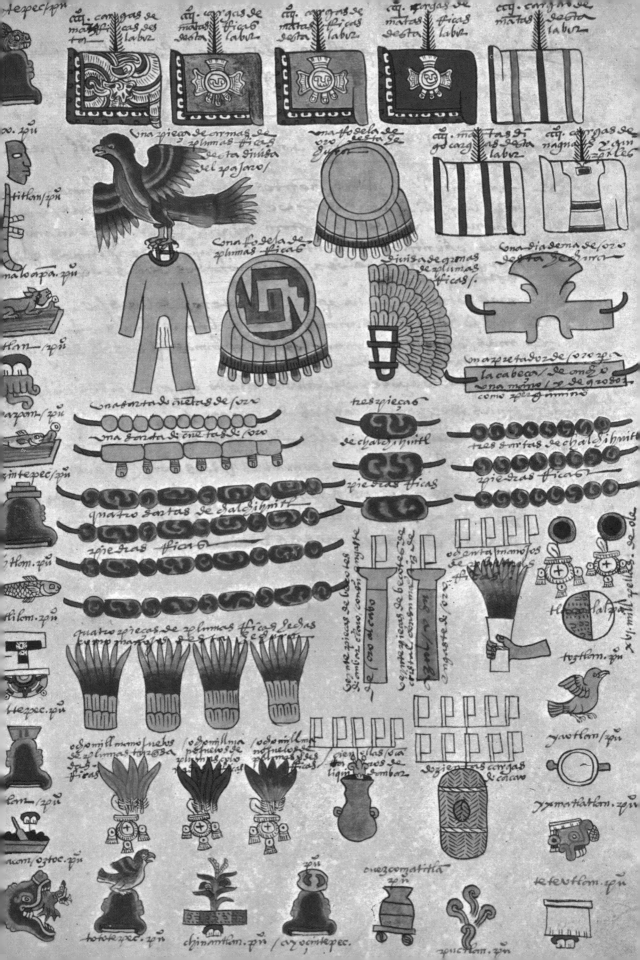

GREAT CITIES, DRENCHED IN BLOOD

Above: As drums beat, Aztec priests lead victims up a pyramid to the temple to be sacrificed. Aztecs believed that unless the state god Huitzilopochtli were appeased by human blood, the sun would fail.

Right: An Aztec priest, having cut the heart from a living victim, offers it to the sun god Tonatiuh. The Spaniards found 136,000 human skulls at the temple in Tenochtitlán, modern Mexico City.

Opposite page: Quetzalcoatl, god of the morning star, played a part in the conquest of Mexico. Aztecs believed he was white and would return one day; when Hernando Cortez arrived, they at first welcomed him, mistaking him for the god.

In April of 1519, Hernando Cortez landed 600 soldiers on the east coast of Mexico, burned his boats so none could turn back, and went to Tenochtitlán, gleaming capital of the Aztec empire. Half believing that Cortez was Quetzalcoatl, the emperor Montezuma—represented (left) by the feathered glyph beneath his near-nude messenger—sent gifts to halt the attack. Instead, Cortez took Montezuma into custody while his troops took the city. Revolt flared, and in 1521 they had to retake it. Cortez himself, wounded, had to be fished out of a canal by a native ally (above). With a ridiculously tiny army he had conquered a land larger than Spain, and one brimming with wealth.

THE SPANISH CONQUEST

THE WHITE GOD COMES TO CONQUER

THE VICTORS' SPOILS

The Spanish acquired huge wealth from the Indians' rich treasuries or from the mines that they operated, such as the large one (above) in Potosi, in what is now Bolivia. In this 1584 picture, the raw metal is brought by llamas to the refinery (foreground) to be processed.

An example of the Spaniards' brutal treatment of the Indians is shown above in a painting from an Aztec petition of 1570.

Silver ore is being smelted in Mexico in the picture at the right. It was painted by Samuel de Champlain between 1599–1602.

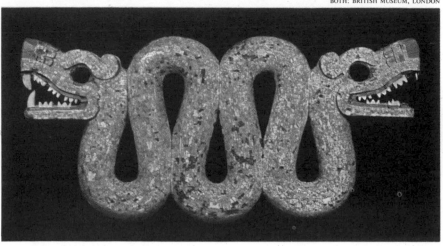

Among the beautiful objects brought home by the conquistadors was a 17½-inch-long ornament of shell and turquoise, perhaps an Aztec fire serpent.

THE SPANISH CONQUEST

THE WEALTH OF THE INDIES

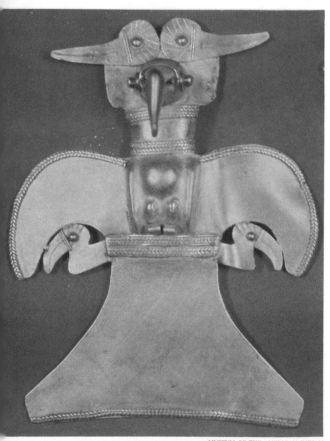

In 1520, the German engraver Albrecht Durer, viewing the presents sent by Montezuma to Charles I, described in his diary "an entire golden sun a full fathom wide, and likewise an entire silver moon equally as large . . . and all sorts of marvelous objects . . . much more beautiful than things spoken of in fairy tales." It is impossible to put a price upon the total booty of the conquistadors. Montezuma's treasures alone were valued by the historian Prescott at $6,000,000. Another 19th-century scholar said the roomful of gold that the perfidious Pizarro demanded for Atahualpa's ransom was worth $20,000,000. And of course there was, in the fabulously rich mines, more where that wealth came from. The gold ornament (left) is from Colombia. The skull (right), overlaid with obsidian and turquoise, probably represents the somber Aztec god Tezcatlipoca.

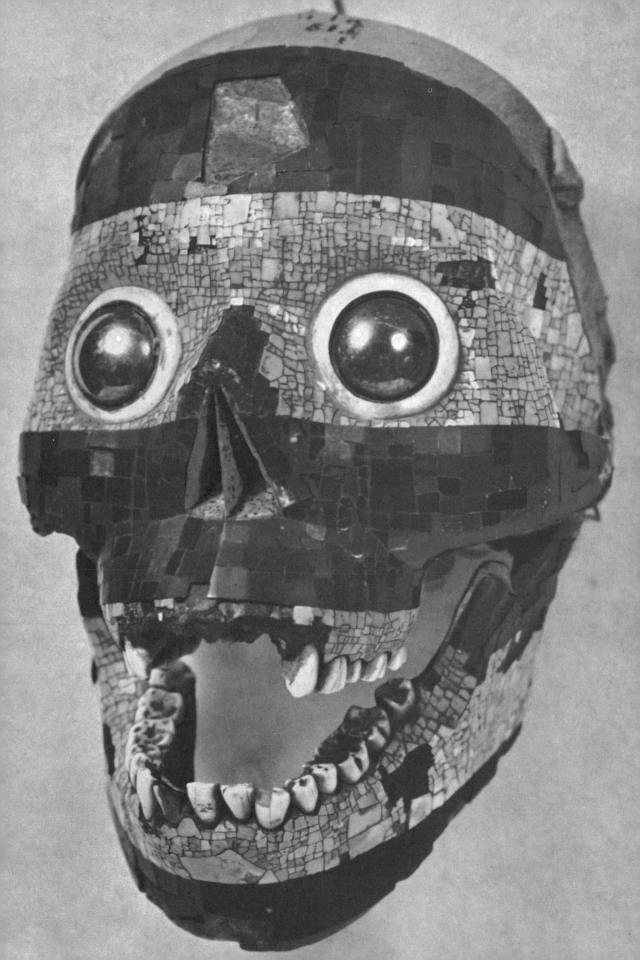

CHAPTER 2

COLONIES FOR ALL

By 1492 there was little evidence to suggest Spain was ready to embark upon worldwide exploration and conquest. The residents of that country had struggled for over 700 years to fight off the incursions of the Moslems, who had invaded in 711. During these bloody centuries, attention was paid wholly to internal affairs; there was hardly a moment to look abroad. In 1402, Henry III of Castile had sent out a small expedition to take control of the offshore Canary Islands, but due to pressures at home no real colonial effort resulted. Such projects were set aside for another 90 years.

Events moved rapidly in 1492, however, and by the middle of that year hopes for expansion were much stronger. The Moslems now were confined to a small area in the southern part of the country, known as Granada, and soon they would be evicted. Already the two principal monarchies of the peninsula were joined in a family union through the marriage of

A Timucua chief in Florida consoles the wives of warriors killed in battle. From a 16th-century eyewitness drawing.

Ferdinand of Aragon and Isabella of Castile. For the time being, each province maintained its own governmental structure, but that distinction would go. With the triumph over the Moors, a large number of unemployed soldiers, hardened from years of campaigning and restless for further excitement, were eager to join in any adventure that might promise fortunes. Reports of breath-taking opportunities in the lands Columbus had discovered gave a driving force from within Spain that sent legions of bold men out on missions of conquest. With a more centralized government, supported by a strong Church, the country was ready to support such individuals. Powered by economic and religious forces, the expansion was bound to bring results.

Within a few years, individual names stood out on the roster of Spanish conquest. The adventures of Hernando Cortez became a legend. He entered Mexico in 1519, and after founding Vera Cruz, quickly fought his way to Mexico City. When that bastion fell, he conquered nearby territory and by 1522 reached the Pacific. While this was happening, Ferdinand

A 16th-century water color shows the army of Cortez marching on Mexico City.

Magellan's fleet not only crossed this great body of water but sailed completely around the world. Vasco de Balboa found the Pacific in 1513 by crossing the Isthmus of Panama, thus providing an entering wedge for Spanish expansion in that area. A little before Cortez was establishing himself firmly in Mexico City and Magellan was on the high seas, Ponce de Leon made the first of his explorations into Florida, in search—as legend claims —of waters reputed to have marvelous powers of rejuvenation. He received an arrow wound on his last trip there and returned to Cuba in 1521 to die. Others carried on his work. In 1528, Cabeza de Vaca moved along the Florida coast and then sailed across the gulf to present Texas, where most of the party was lost. De Vaca and three others turned up years later in Mexico, where they reported the fabulous Seven Cities of Cibola and their gleaming walls. Between the years 1539 and 1543, Hernando De Soto's exploring party of 500 men scoured the present Southeastern states in search of treasure. They found little of material value but gained much geographical knowledge. De Soto died in 1542 as his party descended the Mississippi River, and more than a year later the remnants of the expedition straggled into Mexico.

Accounts brought back by the conquistadors generated further attempts.

The tales arising from de Vaca's journey, for example, so excited the imagination of those at Mexico City that in 1539 a Franciscan friar named Fray Marcos de Niza was sent out with de Vaca's companion Estevanico to investigate. Due to a hostile reception by the Indians, they failed to locate the Seven Cities, but reports of their journey were so exaggerated that in 1540 Francisco Coronado was dispatched upon yet another expedition in the same region. After marching for two years through parts of present Arizona, New Mexico, Kansas, and the Texas Panhandle, this latest adventurer returned, thoroughly disappointed. He found no "fishes as big as horses" or natives whose kitchenware was made of gold, as his guide had promised. But even though he discovered no cities of silver, Spanish geographical knowledge and land claims were increased.

While the various expeditions were being carried on in North America during the years 1520 to 1540, there was an equally feverish search going on in South America. After several unsuccessful attempts to conquer Peru, Francisco Pizarro gained control in 1533. During the next three years he consolidated his gains, with the result that huge amounts of bullion were sent back to Spain. Unfortunately, in Peru, as was true in many other Spanish-conquered areas, the victors fell to fighting among themselves for supremacy, and the early days of the new regime were characterized by internal strife.

Control through monopoly

To achieve any real success in controlling its vast new empire, Spain had to evolve some kind of policy for governing it. One of the first problems confronting the conquistadors was that of the Indian. Historically the Spanish had treated any non-Europeans as barbarians and fit subjects for slavery, and it was not unnatural that Columbus should have taken home some of the natives in bond-

Aztec gold jewelry, including serpent, monkey, owl, and the head of a god.

age. Ferdinand and Isabella decided to take another course with regard to the New World and promised that the Indians would not only be treated kindly but converted to Catholicism. They freed the slaves that Columbus had taken.

It was at Hispaniola (Haiti), the first Spanish colony, that the new system of conversion was put into operation. The natives were divided among the colonists who were to Christianize them and to care for them. This division, which became known as the *repartimiento* (apportionment) system, actually resulted in slavery—although the crown continued to insist that even though the Indians were employed in such a manner, they were free. Isabella seemingly was more interested in the souls of the natives than their earthly existence. Upon her death the more practical Ferdinand came to power, and henceforth the exploitation was open and ruthless. It is not surprising that the result was a sharp rise in the death rate of those who were undergoing the rigors of being "saved."

Aside from control of the native population, the Spanish government lost no time in assuring itself that no other country would share in the exploitation of its newfound wealth. Each ship sailing from Spain carried instructions for collecting all available information for the king. All the mineral resources of the Americas were claimed by the crown. Individuals could work the mineral-bearing lands, but the monarch claimed half, or in some cases one-third, of the yield. However, gold and silver were not considered the only wealth to be realized, and at an early date colonists were urged to take along agricultural tools and seeds. The result was the introduction of wheat, barley, rice, sugar, lemons, olives, grapes, and other products into the Western Hemisphere. Cattle were brought here as early as 1494.

Transportation, another monopoly, was controlled by the use of a fleet of ships that plied back and forth across the Atlantic. It was known as the *flota,* and sailing twice a year with from 40 to 70 ships, this great convoy carried manufactures to America and returned with bullion or raw materials. No other country was allowed any trade with Hispanic America, and a rigid check was kept upon even the licensed traders.

Heretics were kept at home

To guarantee absolute economic control, there was organized in 1503 the *Casa de Contratacion* (House of Trade). It acted as a funnel through which all goods passing between Spain and America, east or west, must go. Ultimately it came to control even human cargo and had the power to say who might go to the colonies. Only the faithful, the most sincere Catholics, were permitted to leave, for there were to be no religious heretics in the new land. Such stringent regulations were necessary if the

These West Indies natives were first offered the opportunity to convert to Christianity, and when they refused, they were mercilessly burned to death.

little nation of Spain, having but 7,000,000 to 8,000,000 people, was to conquer and exercise control over so vast an area as Hispanic America.

The House of Trade worked well enough in bottling up economic potentialities abroad, but so vast was the colonial undertaking that before long some means had to be devised to keep an eye on the rapidly spreading political structure. In 1524, therefore, Charles I assented to the reorganization of the Council of the Indies. This small board carefully chose every offi-

41

In 1564, Le Moyne, a Frenchman, painted these Florida Indians. He discovered a column with French arms, planted in 1562 and worshiped by the Indians.

cial who was to go to America and kept a close check upon all those who went.

In addition to the Council of the Indies, the crown received help in administrative affairs abroad from representatives directly responsible to the king. These men, called viceroys, were absolute in America. Antonio de Mendoza, the first of them, took office in Mexico in 1535. The viceroy commanded immense respect and obedience and was so powerful that colonial residents were obliged to stand in awe of him, as if he were himself a king. On the economic side, this official was the king's watchdog, and he regularly visited the towns under his command to determine if more revenue could be produced or to see if any hidden treasure was escaping notice. Under him was an officer known as the captain general, who commanded the various subdivisions or districts within the viceroyalty. Although just a petty viceroy, he often communicated directly with the Council of the Indies to provide a check on the activities of his superior. To complete the circle, there was a local court known as the *audiencia*. It comprised usually three judges. This body kept an eye on both the viceroy and captains general and reported any suspicious activities to the monarch himself.

Spanish colonial administration was characterized by extreme control, which helps account for the fact that Spain had colonies in America longer than most of its European neighbors. It also explains in part why once the colonies of Spain had freed themselves, they had difficulty in establishing stable, self-sustaining governments. So long a time under such rigid and centralized control killed much of the initiative seen in the English colonies, where a measure of self-government existed from the outset.

France falls far behind

During the rich years of colonial adventure in the 16th century, when Spain established herself so firmly in the Western Hemisphere, France accomplished little. The French kings of that period desperately fought for complete authority at home and spent so much energy that any effort in America was out of the question. As if the internal difficulties were not enough, the French were unable to resist the lure of an apparently weak but rich Italy, and time after time their troops plunged southward into the peninsula, only to be hurled back. By 1600 the nation was bled dry and bankrupt. It was a sorry country that Henry IV took over in 1589. Roads were in disrepair, bridges destroyed, towns burned or abandoned, and the countryside teemed with plundering soldiers. Thus France was able to do little in America before 1600.

Despite the local turmoil and an inability to exploit colonial finds, and in face of the Spanish protest that the Pope had assigned to them the Western Hemisphere, there were some discoveries and claims made by the French during the apparently fruitless century. Between 1523 and 1543, men like Giovanni da Verrazano and Jacques Cartier carried the flag to North America, and in the two decades that followed, others attempted to found colonies as far south as Florida. When Henry IV came to power, his government at once showed a renewed interest in colonization. French capitalists could now turn their money toward American furs with royal encouragement. Between 1603 and 1615, Samuel de Champlain, the chief founder of New France, made many explorations, and in 1627 helped persuade Cardinal Richelieu, the power behind the French throne, to organize The Hundred Associates, a fur-trading monopoly. As part of the bargain, the company was to transport 4,000 agricultural settlers to the New World within 15 years.

The project was a failure. French Protestants were not allowed to leave the country, and the Catholics, who could, were reluctant. Unlike Spain, there was good farming land yet in France and hence little attraction for farmers in America. The peasant, despite his other difficulties, was attached to his land, and other pressures were not great enough to move him. So the French continued to be interested primarily in furs and not farms in the new country. By 1665 they had only about 3,500 settlers in America as compared to at least 75,000 English.

When Louis XIV, at 23, became the warlike despot of France in 1661, there was a renewed effort at colonization, despite the earlier failure of Richelieu. An earnest effort to gain something useful for the homeland, other than furs, was started. Jean Baptiste Colbert, the king's able minister of finance, tried to copy the English practice of developing colonies as a source of raw materials. The move fitted well into the current theory of economics known as mercantilism. According to that system, each nation tried to gain more gold than it found necessary to spend. Money, as always, was power, and the monarchs sought it ceaselessly. Colonies were regarded as a source of raw materials that could be processed in the mother country and the finished product sold at a profit, thus increasing the nation's supply of bullion.

Under Colbert's guidance, France

New France became a valuable colony 17th-century print—fish caught off the

pursued a policy of restrictiveness similar to that used by the Spanish—excluding foreigners from her colonial commerce and granting monopolies to merchants at home. The scheme worked fairly well in the West Indies. French-made goods were exchanged for tobacco, sugar, cotton, indigo, and other products not raised at home. Settlers in New France were expected to buy from France and in

or the reasons illustrated in this
oast and furs the forests yielded.

turn supply food, lumber, work animals, and other items of trade to the West Indies. Here the plan broke down and the French in the islands were obliged to buy from the English. To stimulate the lagging agricultural efforts in Canada, the French now tried to copy the Spanish system of granting large blocks of land to enterprising individuals. However, unlike the Spanish, who were used to

living under feudalism, with the seigneurs extracting rent and services from their countrymen, few Frenchmen wanted to exchange a position of relative freedom to return to feudalism, in America or anywhere else.

The colonial system of New France also resembled the pattern set by Spain in its type of government. It was one of centralized control, with the governor-general heading not only the armed forces but also civil and diplomatic departments. The familiar system of cross-checks was provided in the intendant, who acted as the king's spy and kept him informed of every development in the colony. In addition, New France had a council made up of the governor-general, the intendant, the bishop of the Church, and five (later 12) councilors appointed by the king. It issued all manner of decrees and was the court of highest appeal in all the French possessions on this side of the Atlantic.

It was quickly apparent that the French system was cursed by the same restrictiveness as that of the Spanish. While it may have been successful in driving off real interlopers, it had a deadening effect that prevented a real and constructive growth. All aspects of daily life were minutely regulated. Besides the trade monopoly enforced by the mother country, there were rules concerning contact between the Indians and whites as well as other personal curbs. As if the governmental controls were not enough, the clergy held a tight rein

45

This Dutch map of 1635 shows the Noord Rivier (the Hudson River), which Henry Hudson sailed up in 1609, seeking the Northwest Passage to the Orient.

over the colonists' moral and religious life. Here, as in New Spain, it was the business of the Church to see that no taint of heresy appeared. Under such scrutiny many a colonist decided to move westward, away from control and restriction. The population was too sparse to permit much spread, and in the end the process weakened New France.

Late as they were in the business of expansion, the French, like the Spanish, gained control of a large area. But they were unable to dominate it so well. The northern Indian tribes were

nomadic, decentralized, and devoid of a form of government like that seen in Central America. The absorption of large groups of these Indians was a physical impossibility. Nor were economic opportunities so great as in South America. The Indians had no large amount of treasure, the climate was cold, and the variety of near-tropical products available farther south could not be produced here. Faced by vast distances, a forbidding land, and poor transportation facilities, the French came by a sprawling empire that produced little for them. Their total impression upon the New World, therefore, was considerably less than that of the Spanish or the English.

Unsuccessful imitators

In North America it was the English, and not the French or other European powers, who finally became dominant. The main challenge to the final winner came from four great Continental powers—Spain, France, Holland, and Sweden. While the French held a shaky grip on Canada, and Spain pushed up from the south, it was the Dutch who posed an immediate threat by planting a colony right in the middle of England's holdings. Holland, a rising commercial country in the 17th century, sent Henry Hudson on the same quest that all others sooner or later embarked upon —the discovery of a waterway across North America. In 1609 he sailed up a broad and encouraging-looking river that was to carry his name, and while he did not come out on the Pacific, he did lay claim to an important section of land. By 1624, the Dutch West India Company had dispatched people to America, and settlement of the Hudson River Valley had begun. Like the French, the Dutch were admittedly interested in the fur trade. New Amsterdam (New York) was established on the coast and Fort Orange (Albany) was built upriver as a fur-trading outpost. Flanked by forts on the Delaware and Connecticut Rivers,

Hudson went with his ship, the Half Moon, *for 150 miles up the river bearing his name. The Indians (below), seen staring at his ship, greeted him with generosity and traded beaver and otter skins for beads, knives, and hatchets.*

a small colonial empire made ready to establish a lucrative trade in valuable pelts.

During its existence of only 40 years, New Netherland grew slowly. It was hard to get Dutch burghers to leave comfortable homes in Holland. Blessed with religious toleration and a favorable agricultural system, few wanted to exchange them for life under the managers of large estates in America. The land system here, somewhat like that of Spain and France, featured control by aristocrats called patroons. They ruled over European tenants who worked the land. Despite the unpopularity of the system, it left its mark upon the American scene by establishing a social cleavage in New York that remained powerful until the 1830s. Like the French and Spanish systems, that of the Dutch was restrictive and centralized, allowing for little self-government. Officials sent out from Holland were superimposed upon the people, and organizations like the Dutch West India Company exercised far more control than many an emigrant liked.

As the Dutch colony struggled for a permanent place, nestled dangerously in English territory, the Swedes attempted to establish themselves on the shores of Delaware Bay. Fort Christina was built in 1638 on the site of present Wilmington. The colony never amounted to over 400, and in 1655 the Dutch conquered it. Within 10 years (by 1664) the English in turn took over the Dutch holdings and then turned on France.

America—a pawn of Europe

The American colonies of various European powers were pawns in a larger game. As the mercantile system developed, intense commercial rivalries grew in Europe, and the result was a race for power both at home and abroad. The long-range result was the weakening of the home government and an inability to press its colonial efforts further. Small but determined England gradually forged ahead in the contest with Spain, checkmating her more successfully than any other nation did. And even in Hispanic America there were great inroads made by the hard-fighting Elizabethan English, who by open war or covert smuggling chipped away at the Spanish holdings.

Of the several European powers holding to the theory of strict colonial control, Spain was best able to maintain its position in America. One by one, Sweden, Holland, and France lost out. But even the Spanish, with a complex and highly restrictive system, could not keep ideas from filtering into their colonies. Rule by arbitrary monarchs in a faraway land was hard to fix firmly upon an enormous American empire. When these distant kings fought one another at home and involved their colonies in expensive wars, the possibility of cutting loose from home ties became increasingly attractive to men in America.

THE PILGRIMS' EUROPE

England at the turn of the 17th century was a land of sharp contrasts. Great wealth came to some people from the new and booming colonial trade; abject poverty came to others with the collapse of the feudal landholding system. The Church of England was opposed by the rebellious new Protestant sects that wanted to worship in their own way. Under Queen Elizabeth (above) the island kingdom became a colonial and merchant nation. Her successor, James I, who ruled from 1603 to 1625, failed to improve the lot of his subjects in the rural areas and also denied even the modicum of religious freedom Elizabeth had tolerated. It was during his reign that the Separatists—largely country people opposed to the state church—made their pilgrimage to Holland and then to America. Scenes of the England they left, and the Holland where they first sought refuge, are illustrated in this portfolio.

49

ELIZABETHAN LONDON

In the Pilgrims' day, London Bridge—shown above in 1639—was a bustling center for merchants and craftsmen. Goods from many distant lands were sold in the shops that lined the bridge, and the traders were eager for new markets. Seventy Merchant Adventurers from this section formed the company that financed the voyage of the Pilgrims.

The Englishmen at the right played major roles in the life of William Brewster, the Pilgrim who acted as religious leader of the Plymouth Colony. As a boy of 16, Brewster worked as a valet to Sir William Davison, a diplomat at the court of Queen Elizabeth. Both Brewster and his father worked for the family of Sir Edwin Sandys, who did much to help the Separatists gain permission to colonize.

SIR EDWIN SANDYS

SIR WILLIAM DAVISON

51

THE PILGRIMS' EUROPE

MERRIE ENGLAND

The England that the Separatists were so eager to leave behind had its gay and happy moments, as seen in this 1590 painting, *Wedding Feast at Bermondsey,* by Joris Hoefnagel. The building in the background, across the Thames, is the famous Tower of London.

RURAL BEGINNINGS

The Separatist movement began in the peaceful English countryside, and some of its historic landmarks can be seen there today. William Bradford, who was to be governor of the Plymouth Colony, was born at Austerfield in an old stone farmhouse (right). While still a boy, he turned against the Church of England practices in the Austerfield parish church (above); instead he attended the unconventional services of Richard Clyfton in nearby Babworth. Clyfton, who was to shape Bradford's religious thinking, led a handful of country people in the kind of religious observance that was to become the rule in the Plymouth Colony.

BOTH: JOHN BULMER

William Brewster abandoned his parish church, St. Wilfred's in Scrooby (above), to go to the same services at Babworth that young Bradford attended. Brewster's job as postmaster of Scrooby Post House (foreground) was taken from him in 1607 because of his religious activities.

PILGRIM HALL.

In this 16th-century cartoon, a Puritan minister, reading the Bible from a pulpit, has his beard tweaked by an opposing religionist.

THE PILGRIMS' EUROPE

RELIGIOUS PERSECUTION

The Anabaptist.   The Brownist.

The Familist.   The Papist.

The Separatists who came to America were not the only people in opposition to the Church of England in the 17th century. Four groups at odds with the state church are shown (left) tossing the Bible in a blanket. Three radical Protestant sects—the Brownists, the Anabaptists, and the Familists—are included, as well as the Papists (Roman Catholics).

A Church of England gathering, held in the courtyard of London's St. Paul's Cathedral in 1618, is shown at the right. Government control and approval of the proceedings is indicated by the presence of King James I, with his family, in the elevated royal box in the center.

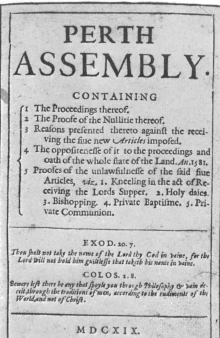

PERTH ASSEMBLY.

CONTAINING

1 The Proceedings thereof.
2 The Proofe of the Nullitie thereof.
3 Reasons presented thereto against the receiving the fiue new *Articles* imposed.
4 The oppositenesse of it to the proceedings and oath of the whole state of the Land. *An.* 1581.
5 Proofes of the unlawfulnesse of the said fiue Articles, *viz.* 1. Kneeling in the act of Receiving the Lords Supper. 2. Holy daies. 3. Bishopping. 4. Private Baptisme. 5. Private Communion.

EXOD. 20. 7.

Thou shalt not take the name of the Lord thy God in vaine, for the Lord will not hold him guiltlesse that taketh his name in vaine.

COLOS. 2. 8.

Beware lest there be any that spoyle you through Philosophy & vain deceit, through the traditions of men, according to the rudiments of the World, and not of Christ.

MDCXIX.

By August of 1608 all of William Brewster's stalwart little band of English Separatists had arrived in Holland, the strange new land shown in the winter scene above. The future Pilgrims enjoyed the novelty of the canals and windmills, but the Dutch language and customs were hard for them to learn or even to understand. William Brewster, who became a printer in Leyden, Holland, found himself again in trouble with the British authorities when he ran off the tract at the left. The *Perth Assembly* was an attack on King James I for trying to force the Scotch Presbyterians to accept the authority of the Church of England. In 1620, having finally got permission to establish a colony in the New World, the English Separatists left Holland in the *Speedwell* (right). They were setting sail on the first leg of a difficult journey to a land and life unknown to them.

THE PILGRIMS' EUROPE

REFUGE IN HOLLAND

At Plymouth (above), the Separatists from Holland joined with those recruited in England. With little hope of ever seeing their homeland again, they boarded the *Mayflower,* seen riding at anchor in the harbor.

ON TO AMERICA

The uncompromising, arrogant James I of England, seen at the left in his most elegant royal costume, was unwilling to allow his subjects to worship as they pleased. To the Puritans' demand for "liberty of conscience" he said, "I will make them conform themselves or I will harry them out of the land."

At the right is the only surviving and authentic known portrait of a passenger on the 1620 voyage of the *Mayflower.* It is a painting of Edward Winslow, who once worked with William Brewster at his press in Leyden. Winslow, founder of a famous New England family, sat for the artist during a visit to England in 1651.

61

CHAPTER 3

THE ENGLISH COLONIES

Anyone studying the expansion of European nations in America may ask, "Why did England succeed so admirably when she entered the colonial race so late?" The Portuguese were hard at work exploring more than 200 years before the Jamestown settlement was established in 1607. By that date the Spanish were thoroughly entrenched in the New World, spreading their power throughout South and Central America, Mexico, and well into the present southwestern United States. Sir Francis Drake circumnavigated the globe 50 years after Magellan showed the way. Even the French preceded the English in America by planting a colony at Port Royal, Nova Scotia, in 1605.

Historian Charles A. Beard suggested some of the answers. England, being an island, was protected from the ravages of European armies and could spend defense funds for a navy rather than a large army. This made it possible not only to defend the homeland but also to send ships far

Sir Walter Raleigh, poet and statesman under Elizabeth and James I, organized some of the early expeditions to America.

across the world to establish and protect colonies. At an early date England's naval power soared to worldwide notice. By 1588 it would sweep the Spanish invaders out of the English channel, and then set about chasing away the Dutch and bottling up the French navy.

Rivalries on the Continent were another factor that worked in favor of England. While Europeans pounded one another with body blows which resulted in a loss of men and resources, England stood aloof, preserving her strength and always holding the balance of power. As France futilely fought Holland (which received just enough English aid to fight back), thousands of French and Dutch soldiers died who might have been colonists. Further blood was let as France tore herself to pieces with the wars of religion in the latter half of the 16th century, fought with Spain over spoils in Italy, and participated in a general European quarrel known as the Thirty Years War. There was no possibility that Germany or Italy would try to colonize, for these countries as we know them did not exist until the 19th century. During the intervening years the organized nations of Europe fought over them in quest of spoils, while, in general, England looked on. From time to time the English participated, when and where it would avail them of something useful, but more often they stood back and watched their sister countries on the Continent undo themselves.

Another reason the English were successful in America was the inconsistency of their rivals. In particular the Dutch and French—both nations of shrewd traders—failed to make a unified effort in colonizing America. For a period of years they would work hard at it; then as wars broke out at home, the colonial effort would lag. Already mentioned is the fact that the French were narrow in their policies toward the colonies. Their refusal to let the Huguenots emigrate to the New World is illustrative. Spain was no less guilty. Despite initial economic success, it was essentially a feudal and clerical land. There was little manufacturing and almost no middle class to act as a commercial backbone. Like that of the French and Dutch, the Spanish policy was essentially restrictive and exploitive so far as America was concerned.

Were the English more successful than their rivals simply because of an abundance of sea power and an ability to exploit a political balance of power in Europe? There were other factors involved. The colonization of English North America was carried out by an essentially civilian group, privately financed and led by self-appointed administrators. It was the beginning of America's much talked-of private enterprise and rugged individualism of a later day. While it was more a corporate undertaking than individual, and was controlled by governmental regulations in England, there was less direct participation by the home government than in rival colonies.

The feminine influence

Another farsighted practice of the English was to bring along their women. This made for a more homogeneous society than that of the French and Spanish colonies, in which men took native wives. And it also meant the family unit was to provide a solid core for a racially well-knit people, who early indicated that they had come to stay. For the next 300 years, as the descendants of these early settlers pushed westward across the continent, building the nation, it was the presence of the women and of the unit that provided stability and permanence to the new communities. It was they who demanded schools, religion, and order. It was their presence that encouraged a cultural uplift and broke down some of the roughhouse tendencies of the masculine frontier. While the Spanish and French ranged over vast stretches of land, unhampered by any family ties, except momentary domesticity with occasional native women, the English

The English triumph over the Spanish Armada in 1588 put an end to the efforts of Philip II of Spain to annex England to his empire—by force or by marrying Elizabeth. This idealized portrait was painted after his death by Rubens.

Henry VIII

stayed close to home. The result was a family type of frontier, characterized by small farms, that remained much more compact, more easily defended, and permanent in nature.

If the colonial methods employed by England account for her success, her preparation at home for such a venture must not be overlooked. By 1600 she had moved farther away from the system of feudalism than any of her Continental neighbors. There was no dominant military clique, and the monopolistic clergy, once the owner of large land holdings, had been deprived of considerable power. As these forces diminished on the national scene, there arose a strong merchant class. It produced a number of small, independent capitalists, ready and willing to project their efforts anywhere in the world in search of profit.

A by-product of this business growth was the emergence of responsible government and constitutional law. The merchants, orderly and regular in their conduct, demanded the same from the government. An arbitrary monarch, always greedy for funds and accustomed to wielding the mace of taxation when and where he felt like it, could not be a part of this system. The merchant class demanded that the king be responsible to his government and made the demand stick. This group of businessmen were becoming more secular than religious in their thinking, more interested in the credit rating than the religious beliefs of their friends. Naturally the pressure of business interests tended to relax earlier religious intolerance.

In order to take advantage of world-wide commercial possibilities, Englishmen began to combine their assets in the form of trading companies. Corporate effort proved to be much more successful than individual attempts. In 1555, the first of the major English trading companies, the Muscovy Company, was chartered to trade with Russia. And in Elizabeth's reign, charters were granted to the Levant Company, which broke into the Italian trade monopoly of the Near

East, and to the East India Company, which stretched its tentacles to the Ganges in India, forcing its way into the Portuguese concessions there. Thus, when the possibility of planting a colony in North America presented itself, the English were quite at home in the formation of corporations for just such an adventure. With no difficulty the London Company and the Plymouth Company were organized in 1606.

Why Englishmen left home

If conditions in France, Holland, and Sweden were good enough to discourage people from exchanging their old homes for new, such was not the case in England. The disappearance of serfdom, gradual as it was, resulted in unemployment for thousands of peasants who had for years quietly farmed under the feudal system. The change did not necessarily arise out of humanitarian sentiments of the masters. The old system proved to be unprofitable in a money economy, and many a landlord was glad to free his land of the peasants who ate up his produce. The owners were eager to convert their lands into some kind of cash crop. Sheep raising had become popular as the demand for wool by Flemish weavers across the channel grew. Thousands of acres were now fenced off by hedges, and the great enclosures, as they were called, became the order of the day. Estates that had once employed large numbers of workers now needed only a few sheepherders; an unprecedented agricultural unemployment resulted.

To make it all worse, about this time a large amount of land was taken from the Catholic Church as Henry VIII broke with that institution. The new masters, bent upon making the greatest profit in the shortest time, enclosed the land and threw even more farmers out of work. Thus by the time of Elizabeth (1558) droves of unemployed roamed the highways. England's pauper population grew and debtors filled the prisons. The newly freed serfs found that their escape from bondage was a questionable boon, and any opportunity was

Flemish farmers in the 16th century were content to stay home and work in the fields.

taken to leave England. The price of a passage to America was to become an indentured servant, another type of bondage, but as there was little alternative, thousands went.

England's religious situation provided another, although less important, reason for moving. During the 1540s, Henry VIII had broken with the Catholic Church at Rome, and through the next 20 years there was a confused struggle to see if the nation would be predominantly Catholic or Protestant. At the time Elizabeth came to the throne, the answer appeared to be the latter. A few years later, with the adoption of the Thirty-nine Articles and certain supplementary measures, England became Anglican Protestant. Since the reign of Henry VIII, the church had been governed by an archbishop who received his appointment from the monarch, thus assuring governmental control of the religious hierarchy. Many Catholics believed that the newly established Church of England would bring no fundamental changes other than a physical separation from Rome. Indeed, the new church preserved a large part of the Catholic ritual and beliefs, modified only by a strong Calvinistic theological tinge.

As in every society, there were those who did not think the reforms far-

This 17th-century Spanish map shows the ports from Guatemala to California looted by Thomas Cavendish in 1587, along the path of Sir Francis Drake's raids in 1579.

68

reaching enough. They wanted to "purify" the church by eliminating more of the old Catholic ritual. They came to be called Puritans. Another group, the Separatists, more radical in

belief than any of the others, wanted to get away completely from the notion of an established church. Both the Puritans and Separatists complained so much to King James I, insisting that they be allowed to worship in their own churches in their own way, that he lost his temper and announced that the dissidents must conform or be driven

Three English raiders—Sir John Hawkins, Sir Francis Drake, and Thomas Cavendish.

from the land. Despite these blustering words, a law designed to stop the emigration of nonconformers had been in effect since 1598. All who wished to leave England must get a license from the king. But, in 1617, ailing Jamestown needed colonists so desperately that James I agreed to allow the Separatists to go to the New World. England, like her Continental neighbors, was also to have her heretics. But her desire to colonize the New World was more overriding than that of her neighbors.

One of the most important results of England's commercial growth was the emergence of a large and powerful fleet. In early times there was no great difference between men of war and merchantmen; unlike those of today, commercial vessels could easily be converted into fighting ships by the addition of firepower and other modifications. By the reign of Elizabeth, England had already become a formidable sea power; that fact was demonstrated to the world when in 1588 the Spanish attempted to invade the British Isles.

Yet, while others were busy colonizing, Englishmen momentarily neglected claims made for them in America by such men as John Cabot. As the leading Protestant power, they seemed content to contest the claims of Catholic nations like Spain and Portugal. John Hawkins and Francis Drake led others in this naval hamstringing operation, striking continually at the Spanish monopoly in particular. Hawkins raided that preserve as early as 1562 by engaging in the slave trade and selling Negroes in Hispanic America in direct violation of the law that forbade the colonists to trade with any nation but Spain. Drake, another Protestant, regarded it his duty to lash out at Roman Catholic sovereigns, and under the guise of such a worthy cause he launched himself upon a semi-piratical career at sea. Spanish ships and seaports suffered heavily from his hit-and-run raids, and this was at a time when England and Spain were at peace. To punish him for such transgressions, Queen Elizabeth shared Drake's loot and made him a knight.

As the 17th century neared, England made ready to enter the colonial

Queen Elizabeth's courtiers are shown carrying their unmarried ruler on a throne to the wedding of Anne Russell, one of her ladies in waiting.

game. In 1583, Sir Humphrey Gilbert sailed to America and tried to plant a colony at New Foundland. He hoped to start with a settlement along what was believed to be the Northwest Passage—the long-sought waterway to Asia—and thus gain commercial advantage on what would be a vital trade route. No doubt the fishermen, who had been drying fish there for possibly a hundred years, listened with surprise as Gilbert gravely read to them a patent issued by the queen that directed him to discover fresh lands. This ceremony over, he packed up a piece of New Foundland turf, formalizing his accomplishment, and headed for England. The adventurer was lost at sea on the way home and his rights reverted to a half brother,

Sir Walter Raleigh. In 1584 this more famous colonizer sent forth an exploring party that spent two summer months scouting the South Atlantic seaboard.

So favorable were the reports that in the following year 108 colonists crossed the Atlantic to take possession of "heathen lands" and to find gold. A most important section of the patent granting them permission to settle on Roanoke Island on Albemarle Sound extended the same privileges as those given to the Englishmen at home. The queen was so impressed by what she had heard of the new location that she suggested it be named Virginia after her, the "virgin queen." The new residents were somewhat less enthusiastic about the place, however, and in 1586 when Sir Francis Drake stopped by to see how they were getting on, they all asked for and were granted passage home.

In 1587, another group, this time 116 in number, was sent back to Roanoke Island for a new try at establishing a permanent colony. Because of the Spanish Armada's attempt to storm the island bastion that was England, and for other reasons, no support reached the little settlement until 1591. The crew of the relief ship searched, but no sign of the settlers was found.

As the 16th century drew to a close, England had not yet established herself on the coast of North America. While colonizing in North Carolina lagged, new attempts were being made to the north. In 1605, Captain George Weymouth landed on the coast of Maine, hopeful of finding a suitable location, but he turned up nothing of interest except a few natives. Unwilling to go home empty-handed, he captured five of them, and before they reached England, he had taught them enough English to talk of the fine climate and rich resources in America. Few modern realtors could top this feat.

Despite such failures, men of England indicated a strong interest in the new land, and since their charters usually provided that Englishmen might carry their privileges and liberties abroad, further attempts were bound to follow. Materially, they had brought home only the white potato and tobacco. Sir Ralph Lane, governor of Raleigh's first colony, introduced the potato to his Irish estate, and it was Raleigh himself who popularized smoking with the new brown leaf. Small as were these contributions, they were later to affect commercial Europe mightily. Meanwhile, Spain entered her second century of successful colonial adventure in America; already she was fabulously rich in silver and gold.

The failure of early efforts in Virginia indicated that the task was too big for individual enterprise. The hazards were too great and the cost too high. It was here that Englishmen,

The tattooed Florida warrior carries a quiver of arrows and a bow over six feet long.
BRITISH MUSEUM, LONDON

72

An engraving of John Smith, from his book about his 1614 New England voyage.

accustomed to sharing risks by corporate organization, successfully applied the method to America. Virginia presented a challenge to those at home; groups of merchants glimpsed opportunity abroad and were ready to act. The Spanish had found gold in America, and it was supposed that the English could also. But if bullion could not at once be uncovered, perhaps other wealth could be had by discovering a waterway across the continent. Innumerable river mouths along the coast looked promising. The government was willing to back any ventures along the Atlantic seaboard, for it was now prepared to contest Spain's claim to a large share of North America. Mercantile England was rapidly expanding, and the demand for raw materials grew daily. No European country except Holland was now more interested in a source of supply for its workshops. Great as

were the strides in commerce and industry, unemployment resulting from the enclosures mounted to a point where the government sought a place for its people to overflow. And for those who were unhappy over the religious differences at home, America would be a fine place, too.

Not until 1603 was there a real prospect that Virginia would at last become a permanent settlement. In that year Sir Walter Raleigh was stripped of his colonizing rights, and the way was cleared for a company to take over. When peace came with Spain in 1604, there was further stimulation for the venture. Two years later James I issued charters to two groups of merchants, authorizing them to establish two settlements in America, each of which would comprise 10,000 square miles of land. The Plymouth Company's preserve lay somewhere between latitudes 38°N. and 45°N., and the London Company was assigned the region between latitudes 34°N. and 41°N. In granting the charters, the government did not surrender the right to govern the colonies. A council, appointed by the king, was to sit in England and supervise, while a local council appointed by this body would carry on day-to-day affairs in America. The colonial council had to abide by English laws and was prohibited from passing laws affecting life and limb. Otherwise, it was self-governing. Under this arrangement, the English settlement of North America went ahead.

Powhatan appears in John Smith's 1631 edition of the Generall Historie of Virginia.

The London Company got a head start on the Plymouth Company and in 1607 established what would be the first permanent English town in the present United States. It was named Jamestown, in honor of the king, and American real estate got off to a fast start as John Smith avowed that "heaven and earth never agreed better to frame a place for man's habitation." The original 105 settlers would soon question this extravagant claim, but for the present they could do little but assault the many problems that faced them in the American wilderness.

Complexities of rooting a civilization on a virgin land soon became apparent. Along with the to-be-expected pioneer hardships, the Jamestown settler had to learn to live with the Indian. Powhatan, the powerful chief of the Algonquians, earnestly worked for peace with the Englishman, but Jamestown did suffer sneak attacks by one or another of the villages in Powhatan's confederacy. Yet, despite these sporadic uprisings (sometimes incited by the Spanish to the south), peaceful coexistence was the rule during the difficult early years of the Virginia colony.

As if the external troubles were not enough, however, the men of Jamestown had their own quarrels. The seven-man local council included such strong personalities as Edward-Maria Wingfield and John Smith, and their violent quarrels resulted in division and suffering for all residents. Even more threatening to the little settlement was the incidence of disease. So prevalent was sickness that despite the arrival of two additional groups of people in 1608, the population declined. When in January, 1608, a fire destroyed most of Jamestown's buildings and shortly thereafter rats devoured much of the remaining corn supply, the probability of a permanent settlement in America took a turn for the worse.

The "gentlemen" go on strike

Moreover, there were times when the settlers seemed to be working against their own interests. Some of them took the position that as "gentlemen" they should not work with the soil, but ought to spend their time looking around for precious metals. Some of the other gentlemen preferred not to engage in any labor at all. Meanwhile, in England, the London Company was overanxious for immediate monetary return. Twice during 1608, when vessels arrived in America, the colonists had to stop their building and supply lumber, pitch, tar, and other cargo for shipment home. Precious time was lost, and the much-needed preparations for protection against Indians and a long winter were delayed.

Before long there were loud protestations. Out of the bickering, and despite a number of examples of rugged individualism on the part of the settlers, John Smith managed to gain recognition as the leader. Under his guidance some of the gentlemen found themselves engaged in the ungentlemanly task of cutting down trees. Before long, blistered hands produced a variety of colorful oaths, which Smith answered with a decree that blasphemy would be punished by pouring a can of cold water down the offender's sleeve. While this may have cooled hot tempers, it resulted in more respect than love for the leader, and increased discontent.

Because of complaints from those in America and a fading interest in England, the company decided to liberalize the colony's government. Under a new charter of 1609, which greatly enlarged the colony's boundaries, residents were offered stock in

Sir John Popham financed expeditions, as a partner of Sir Ferdinando Gorges.

the company and given an opportunity to pay for it by labor. In addition to the new charter, more supplies were sent out. They were not enough, and Jamestown now faced the "starving time." Settlers were obliged to eat snails, snakes, roots—anything they could find. The crisis passed, and under more severe laws that demanded strict order, the faltering colony once again went forward. A third charter, issued in 1612, granted the London Company even more power to control its colonial project. If it could only find some profitable product to export from America, the whole scheme promised ultimate success. The search was rewarded by the development of tobacco, and with a cash crop for sale,

the Virginians announced they were in business.

While the London Company struggled to establish a colony in Virginia, those at Plymouth, England, had even less success. The land assigned to them lay north of Virginia, in a region devoid of treasure and less conducive to agricultural attempts. In 1607, Sir John Popham and Sir Ferdinando Gorges had tried to plant a colony on the mouth of the Kennebec River in Maine, to no avail. In 1610, a group of Bristol merchants, armed with a charter, sent a group of 39 colonists to New Foundland. Despite the fact that they landed at so promising a place as Cupid's Cove, on Conception Bay, there was no satisfactory population increase and the colony faltered.

Four years later some London merchants hired the well-known Captain John Smith, recently of Virginia, to hunt whales along the North Atlantic coast. While on this assignment he did a little exploring, and after returning home wrote a book called *A Description of New England,* wherein he coined a name. At once a best seller, the book created great excitement about this new land. Sir Ferdinando Gorges, a powerful member of the Plymouth Company, now applied to the king for a patent to explore and settle this much-talked-of area. In giving his permission, the monarch directed that the region be called New England; it lay between 40°N. and 48°N. latitude and extended from sea to sea.

Promoters in the London Company found their colonists in Holland, not in England. They knew that a group of English Separatists, living at Leyden, wanted to settle in America. Before long, one of the promoters, Thomas Weston, had persuaded the Pilgrims, as they became known, to accept his company's offer of trans-

portation to America and land when they arrived. After some delay they sailed, in September of 1620, along with a group of nondissenters who merely sought new homes in America. Just over 100 men, women, and children crowded aboard the *Mayflower,* and it was almost two months before they caught their first glimpse of America. On the trip there had been one death and one birth; the newcomer was appropriately called Oceanus. As the *Mayflower*'s passengers looked upon an arm of land that would be known as Cape Cod, they had reason to be thankful for a successful voyage. Considering the hazards of travel and crowded conditions, they had done well. So well, in fact, that it was decided they should land instead of searching farther southward for a better location.

First popular government

The decision to put ashore on the Massachusetts beach had some far-reaching implications for later Americans. Word spread throughout the ship's company that the landfall lay north of the jurisdiction staked out for the London Company and in effect they were in no man's land. Rather than being discouraged, some of the rougher elements of the London streets saw opportunity and announced that they would not be bound by the authority of the London Company. It was mutiny. The Pilgrim leaders acted promptly to quell such a premature declaration of independence. In solemn council they agreed

Massasoit

PILGRIM HALL

The first document in the New World to assure government by the rule of the majority was the Mayflower Compact, signed on shipboard off the coast of Cape Cod. Percy Moran painted this incident as it may have occurred.

on November 21 that they were now a body politic and that they would frame laws for the protection of their fellow colonists. In the Mayflower Compact, these men set up the first government of the people and by the people in America. Again and again, on later frontiers, men would sit together and formulate rules for temporary guidance until formal law reached them. The Pilgrim Fathers, like their successors, had no notion of political separation from the parent government; they were simply improvising in the face of necessity.

After preliminary explorations ashore, the colonists decided upon a location and named it Plymouth. On Christmas Day they began felling timber for the construction of buildings. By the early months of 1621, a common house flanked by a row of thatch-roofed huts made partly of woven brush and mud appeared on the shores of Plymouth harbor. Then one warm March day the Pilgrims had a visitor. An Indian named Samoset, wearing only a belt, strode into the village. In surprisingly good English (picked up from fishermen to the north), he welcomed the newcomers and promptly asked for beer. His wants satisfied, he disappeared. In a few days he returned with a friend named Squanto, who showed the hopeful farmers a few agricultural tricks. By fertilizing with fish the hills into which the corn kernels were planted, a better crop was assured. Before long the whites became acquainted with other natives, and soon a fur trade sprang up. By fall a thriving commerce had been established and the corn stood high. Assisted by Chief Massasoit and his braves, the Pilgrims held the Thanksgiving feast so well known to Americans of today. After some years of exile in Holland, the little group of English Pilgrims had established themselves on raw and forbidding shores with less suffering than their countrymen at Jamestown had experienced. Before their establishment could be called permanent, however, there would be days of sickness and hunger.

Private enterprise proves itself

Like those colonists in Virginia, the Pilgrims at first tried a cooperative economic system, but within two years they abandoned it. In search of a method with more incentive, they turned to private enterprise, granting an acre of land to each man. The new plan worked well, and the harvest of 1623 was so rich that the first years of hunger were nearly forgotten. Four years later settlers bought out the London capitalists for 1,800 pounds, to be paid in nine installments, and freed themselves of financial control from England.

Between the years when settlements were first established at Jamestown and Plymouth, conditions in England made it desirable for many to seek homes elsewhere. In 1618 the Thirty

Years War began on the Continent, and even though England was not at once involved, the turmoil had a powerful effect upon her expansion in the New World. As the economy experienced a shift-over from old farming methods to the raising of wool for sale in Europe, wartime conditions on the Continent began to hamper the sale of English cloth. With depression settling on the land, taxes became harder to bear and both farmers and

townsmen suffered. The Church grew increasingly insistent in its demands for religious conformity, to the annoyance of the already hard-pressed man on the street. Between 1618 and 1642 (when civil war broke out, making transportation hard to find), emigration from England grew to such proportions that these years are called the period of the great migration. Men and women left England in droves, headed for the mainland of America and also for the small islands in the Caribbean. Many of them were not people of great pioneering spirit and under normal conditions would have remained in their cottages, hopeful of better times. But these were *not* normal times, and the realization that they had nothing to lose and everything to gain sent them to the nearest seaports for passage. It was their resolve that strengthened the hold of the colonies along Atlantic shores.

MAIN TEXT CONTINUES IN VOLUME 2

The Ordeal of Cabeza de Vaca

A SPECIAL CONTRIBUTION BY

THOMAS F. McGANN

Shipwrecked on the coast of Texas in 1528, this indomitable Spanish explorer began an eight-year struggle for existence as he traveled through land unknown to the white man.

A crude boat carrying 40 exhausted Spaniards drifted close to the long Texas beach. "Near the land a breaker took and threw the boat the cast of a horseshoe out of the water. With the violent blow almost all the men, who were like dead, came to themselves and seeing the beach near they began to climb from the boat and crawl on hands and knees to some ravines where we made fire and toasted some corn that we had bought and drank some rain water that we found. The day that we arrived here was the sixth of the month of November." The year was 1528.

Thus Alvar Nuñez Cabeza de Vaca of Jerez, treasurer of the ill-fated Narvaez expedition, which had set out from Spain in June, 1527, with five ships and 600 men to explore and settle the lands between Florida and Mexico, tells how he came with his few remaining companions to the unknown land of Texas. Years before De Soto and Coronado entered what would become the United States, he was to make one of man's great land journeys, cross-

This Frederic Remington painting of de Vaca, bearded and seated between Indians, shows him in the arid land through which he traveled.

ing Texas and Mexico from the Gulf to the Pacific Ocean with two other white men and a Negro slave.

The Narvaez expedition had spent the winter of 1527–28 in Cuba and sailed in the spring for the little-known shores of Florida. On April 14—Holy Thursday—the five vessels anchored at the mouth of what was probably Tampa Bay. Here, the commander, Panfilo de Narvaez, made his most important decision, and so insured the destruction of his expedition. He divided his force, now only 400 men, took 300 of them ashore, and set out northward toward the place which the Indians called Apalache; there, they said, the Spaniards would find much gold. The ships were ordered to run along the coast and meet the men marching by land at a vague rendezvous. That rendezvous was never kept.

Narvaez and the others in the land party struggled along the coast of Florida, battling Indians all the while. When, late in June, they reached Apalache (perhaps near Tallahassee), the Spaniards found a few huts, corn, and hostile natives, but no gold. The invaders pushed inland, but hunger, sickness, and frequent attacks by the Indians made their march a nightmare.

In desperation Narvaez turned back to the coast and called a council. Cabeza writes, "We agreed on a remedy most difficult to execute, which was to make boats in which to depart . . . we knew not how to do this work, nor were there tools . . . but God willed it that one of the company should say that he could make some wooden tubes which, with deerskins, would serve as bellows . . . and we agreed thus to make from our stirrups, spurs, and crossbows . . . the nails, saws, axes, and other tools of which there was such need. We agreed that every third day we would slaughter a horse to be divided among those working on the boats."

On September 20, five boats were ready, each 33 feet long. From palmetto fiber and the horses' tails and manes the men made rope and rigging, and from their shirts, sails. They flayed the horses' legs entire and tanned the skin to make water bottles.

Two days later, they ate the last horse. Leaving behind more than 50 companions, who had died of disease or wounds, some 250 survivors crowded into the vessels and sailed from the place they called the Bay of Horses.

The sea was as perilous as the land. The gunwales of the boats almost awash, their corn supply almost exhausted, the horsehide water carriers rotten and useless, the Spaniards groped westward along the coast, stopping to beg or to fight the Indians for fish and water. Maddened by thirst, some men drank salt water and died. One day the voyagers came to the mouth of a broad river whose current drove the boats away from the shore, but repaid the men with fresh water. It was the Mississippi.

The five boats were blown out to sea by a howling north wind and became separated. Cabeza and his men sailed for four days, until the roaring breakers hurled them upon the Texas shore that early day in November, 1528.

After the castaways had eaten what little corn they had salvaged, Cabeza ordered one of the men, Lope de Oviedo, to survey the country. When Oviedo returned, he reported they were on an island, and "three Indians with bows and arrows were following him and calling to him and he likewise was beckoning them on. Thus he arrived where we were, the Indians remaining a way back."

So, probably a few miles below the present city of Galveston, on a desolate island now joined to the mainland by the sea's powerful action and called Velasco Peninsula, Indians and white men met. This first meeting of Europeans and natives in the Southwest of the United States was peaceful. The Indians brought fish and roots to the starving strangers, receiving trinkets in return. After resting a few days, the Spaniards dug their boat out of the sand, and with much exertion launched it. Two crossbow shots from shore a wave capsized the boat, drowning three men and tossing the rest back upon the beach.

Here the Indians found them once more, and so sad was the plight of the white men that the Indians howled their ritual lamentation. The natives brought the castaways to their huts and warmed and fed them and then danced all night, to the terror of the Europeans, who feared that they were being prepared for sacrifice.

The next day some 50 more Spaniards came into camp. Led by Andres Dorantes and Alonso de Castillo, and including Dorantes' slave, the Negro-Moor Estevanico, these survivors of the expedition had been wrecked a few miles up the beach.

Together the Spaniards agreed to launch the boat of Dorantes and Castillo. The men who had the strength and will might go in it; the others would make their way along the shore.

The boat was launched, but it sank immediately. Marooned without provisions and with cold weather coming, the Spaniards decided to winter on the island. But they picked four men and sent them on down the coast in an effort to reach the Spanish settlements in Mexico.

Cold and stormy weather swept the island; the Indians could catch no fish and dig no roots; the flimsy huts gave no shelter; death came. Five Spaniards living apart in one hut became cannibals, "until only one remained who, being alone, there was no one who might eat him." Of the more than 80 Spaniards who had come to the island, soon only 15 remained alive.

The Spaniards named this place Malhado—Bad Luck Island. But with the help of the Indians, the 15 Europeans survived. These Indians went naked, except for "the women, who covered their bodies somewhat with a wool that grows in the trees." The men were large and well-formed; they pierced their lower lips and sometimes their nipples with

PROBABLE
LOCATION
OF THE
TUNA GROUNDS
WHERE CABEZA
MADE
HIS ESCAPE

TRINITY R.

BRAZOS R.

GALVESTON
ISLAND

CABEZA
SHIPWRECKED

PECOS R.

BIG
BEND

COLORADO R.

RIO
SONORA

"CORAZONES"

NUECES R.

RIO GRANDE

VELASCO
PENINSULA

CABEZA
SPENDS
SIX YEARS AS
AN INDIAN
CAPTIVE,
1528-34

DESERT

RIO
SINALOA

SAN MIGUEL (CULIACÁN),
*Northernmost outpost
of Spanish colonization
on the west coast of Mexico*

WHERE
CABEZA
MET THE
SPANISH
SLAVE
HUNTERS,
1536

PÁNUCO
*(Nearest Spanish
settlement and
the goal of the
Narváez
Expedition's
survivors)*

COMPOSTELA

N

MEXICO
CITY

SCALE

0   100   200   300   MILES

——————— MODERN U.S. STATE BOUNDARIES
■■■■■ CABEZA'S PROBABLE ROUTE

The precise route of Cabeza de Vaca is a puzzle in probabilities, and necessarily so because of the vagueness of the account of the principal witness, Cabeza himself. Many conflicting interpretations of his route exist, some of which are founded upon knowledge of the region and close analysis of Cabeza's narrative, others on local pride and supposition. An example of such controversy is whether or not Cabeza reached New Mexico and Arizona. Although he may indeed have wandered that far north, it now seems much more likely that he turned west somewhere below present-day El Paso. The route indicated on this map is the one considered most probable by the author of this article.

pieces of cane. They treated their children mildly, engaged in prolonged, lachrymose funeral rites, and had taboos against in-laws. Their beliefs involved the foreigners in a practice that was to save the lives of some of the hapless group: "They wished to make us physicians . . ." Cabeza writes. "They cure illness by blowing on the sick, and with that breath and the placing on of hands they cast out the sickness, and they ordered us to do the same and to be useful to them in some way. We laughed at that, telling them that it was a farce and that we did not know how to cure. For this they took away our food until we did as they told us. . . . The manner in which we cured was by blessing them and breathing on them and by praying a Pater Noster and an Ave Maria."

In the spring of 1529, the Spaniards separated. Thirteen survivors (one more had ap-

peared in the winter) started off toward Mexico. Lope de Oviedo and Alaniz remained on Malhado, too weak to travel. Cabeza, who had been taken to the mainland during the winter and who had fallen ill there, also remained behind—the lone white man, as far as he knew, on the vast and unexplored mainland of North America above Mexico.

For Cabeza de Vaca this was the beginning of four years of prolonged hardship. He suffered bad treatment from the Indians and from nature. "I had to get out roots to eat from under the water and from among the reeds where they grew in the ground and from this my fingers were so worn that they bled if a straw touched them." Hunger and cold beset him. At times he was no more than a slave.

To free himself from dependence upon his

Indian masters, Cabeza gradually set himself up as a trader, traveling among the often hostile Indians to exchange the shells, sea beans, and goods from the coast for the skins, ocher, and flints of the interior.

Each year Cabeza returned to Malhado to try to persuade Lope de Oviedo, the only Spaniard left on the island, to depart with him in search of Christians. Not until 1533 did Oviedo agree. He could not swim, but Cabeza managed to get him to the mainland and across the first four rivers. Down the coast they came upon other Indians who told them that farther on there were three men, two of whom looked like the Spaniards. These Indians also knew of the fate of other members of the expedition. All had died of cold or hunger or had been killed by the natives—for sport or in obedience to omens which had come to the Indians in dreams. While Cabeza and Oviedo waited for the other Spaniards, the natives abused them, holding drawn arrows against their chests and telling them that they were going to be killed. Oviedo's courage failed him. He departed for Malhado, and disappeared from history.

Two days later Alonso de Castillo and Andres Dorantes, and Estevanico, his slave, arrived with their Indian masters, and the four men rejoiced much at finding one another alive. For more than a year the three Spaniards and the Negro lived as slaves of the Indians, who fed mainly on roots, but also ate spiders, worms, caterpillars, lizards, snakes, and ant eggs. Though Cabeza describes them as thieves, liars, and drunkards, they were at the same time "a merry people, considering the hunger they suffer." The women did the camp labor.

"Cattle came here," Cabeza says, "and I have seen them three times, and partaken of them. It seems to me that they are the size of those of Spain. They have small horns . . . and very long hair, flocky, like a merino's. Some are tawny, others black, and it seems to me that they have better and fatter meat than those of Spain. From the smaller ones the Indians make blankets to cover themselves, and from the larger ones they make shoes and shields. They come from the north over the land to the coast, spreading out over all the country more than 400 leagues, and along

A 16th-century French sketch of a buffalo based on accounts by explorers like Cabeza de Vaca.

their route and the valleys by which they come, the people who live nearby descend upon them and live off them." Thus, the first description of the American buffalo.

In the summer of 1533, the Spaniards and the Negro were brought by the Indians to the prickly-pear fields (most likely south of San Antonio). Before the prisoners had a chance to escape, the Indians fell to quarreling and took up their lodges and left. The four Christians (for Estevanico was a Christian) were denied by this dispute an opportunity to escape, and were separated once again, to spend another year in captivity.

After the passage of these hard months, the Indians reassembled to gorge on tunas, the purple fruit that grows from the edges of a flat-leaved, spiny cactus. Here the four men learned they were indeed the last survivors of the Narvaez expedition.

Finally, as the moon grew full in September, 1534, the Spaniards and the Moor slipped away from their masters. Shortly they came upon another tribe, the Avavares, who received them well.

Winter was not far off, and the natives told the Spaniards that the country ahead was poor in game and abandoned by the Indians in the cold months. The travelers decided to remain where they were. They stayed with the Avavares for eight months.

In the late spring or early summer of 1535, the wanderers started again on their quest for Mexico. Now the pattern of their lives changed. They had acquired a reputation as medicine men, and as they moved from tribe to tribe, they were met with rejoicing. Perhaps at this stage of their journey they crossed the lower Rio Grande and entered Mexico. They were still lost, and still hundreds of miles from the nearest Spanish settlements to the south at Panuco. But their march took on the character of a triumphal procession. At each village the Indians brought the sick to be cured, and then escorted the travelers to the next settlement.

When the wanderers came in sight of the mountains of northeastern Mexico, they made what seems a strange decision. They turned from the coastal plain and headed inland, away from the direct route to the Spanish settlements. Cabeza gives the reason for this change—fear of the evil disposition of the coastal Indians, in contrast to the good treatment received from the inland tribes. He also hints that these indomitable men swung away to the west and north in search of the riches and fabled cities that had eluded them since they had sailed from Spain eight years earlier.

Perhaps also they took pleasure in their prosperity and power. Laden with gifts, which they distributed as fast as they were received, and exercising such authority over the awed and superstitious Indians that none dared to take a drink of water without permission from the strangers, the four wandered on.

Along river valleys and across mountain ridges they went west and northwest through northern Mexico. The land was rugged and dry, except in the verdant valleys. In this country the travelers were given corn flour. And Cabeza worked a true cure (of his other "cures," he was always careful to point out that the Indians *believed* they had been cured). He operated on an Indian who had been shot by an arrow, removed the arrowhead from deep in the man's chest, and with a deer bone as a needle sewed up the wound.

Now they had roast quail and venison to eat. On they went, crossing "a great river," probably the Rio Grande again, near the Big Bend. Then, after journeying 250 miles through dry, rough country, they again forded "a very large river," having come back once more to the Rio Grande, farther north. Here they saw houses rather than huts, and the Indians gave them corn, pumpkins, and beans.

The years had hardened the four men physically and confirmed them in their faith: "We used to walk all day without eating until night, and we ate so little that the Indians were astonished to see it. . . . We passed through a great many peoples of diverse tongues; with all of them Our Lord God favored us."

Week after week they walked westward from the Rio Grande, across northwestern Mexico, over the passes of the Sierra Madre, down the western mountain valleys toward the coast, into a land of relative plenty. The Indians brought the Spaniards corals from the Gulf of California and turquoises from the pueblo country of Arizona and New Mexico. The wanderers made their way south, threading the valleys between the mountains and the ocean. Now, news about other Christians became frequent, but it was bad news, at least for the Indians. A Spanish slaving expedition had left the fertile countryside deserted, the villages burned, and the remaining inhabitants hidden in the mountains. Still the Indians who had come with the four travelers continued to journey on, assured by Cabeza of his protection. One morning near the Petatlan River (now the Sinaloa), Cabeza "came upon Christians on horseback, who received a great shock to see me, so strangely dressed and accompanied by Indians. . . . I told them to bring me to where their captain was . . . and I asked him to give me a certificate of the year and the month and the day on which I had arrived there and the manner in which I came, and thus it was done."

By the Sinaloa River, not far from the Pacific Ocean and about 100 miles north of the border settlement of San Miguel, the odyssey of Cabeza, Dorantes, Castillo, and Estevanico ended. The Indians accompanying the "gods" did not wish to abandon them until they had been conveyed into the safekeeping of other Indians, nor did these Indians wish to lose their protectors, for fear of the other white men.

Cabeza relates that the slave-hunting Christians "took offense at this and made their interpreter tell the Indians that we were people of no account, and that they were the lords of that land, who had to be obeyed and served. . . . The Indians said that the Christians lied, because we came from where the sun rises, and they whence it sets; that we healed the sick, while they killed the sound; that we came naked and barefooted, while they came clothed and on horses and with lances; and that we were not covetous of anything, while the others had no aim but to rob everything."

Cabeza finally persuaded the Indians to return to their homes and fields, and he thanked them and dismissed them in peace. With an escort, the four travelers started on their way to Mexico City. But their efforts to protect the natives from the slave hunters had endangered their own lives. Only the arrival of a well-disposed higher official saved Cabeza and the others from possible death at the hands of their own countrymen.

From the border settlement of San Miguel they pushed on 300 miles to Compostela, then another 500 miles to Mexico City. There they were joyfully received and honored by the viceroy, Mendoza, and by the conqueror, Cortez. The harsh imprint of their journey was still upon them, for Cabeza tells that it was some time before he could stand the touch of clothes upon his body, or sleep anywhere but upon the ground.

Cabeza reached Spain the following summer, but by 1540 he was again in the New World, now as governor of Paraguay. Political difficulties led to his recall and imprisonment; he returned to Spain and obscurity until his death, perhaps in the 1550s.

Castillo and Dorantes settled in Mexico.

It was the Negro Christian from North Africa, Estevanico, who died like the conquistador he was. Incited by the rumors of civilizations and treasures in the unknown lands to the north of the regions crossed by Cabeza and his companions, Viceroy Mendoza sent out an expedition led by Fray Marcos de Niza. Its guide was Estevanico. He was killed in 1539 by Indians in the pueblo country of New Mexico, having blazed the trail that would be followed, a year later, by Coronado.

Thomas F. McGann is professor of Latin American history at the University of Texas; author of Argentina, the United States and the Inter-American System, 1880–1914; *and co-editor of* The New World Looks at Its History.

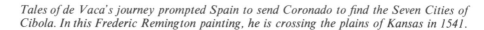

Tales of de Vaca's journey prompted Spain to send Coronado to find the Seven Cities of Cibola. In this Frederic Remington painting, he is crossing the plains of Kansas in 1541.

FOR FURTHER READING

CHAPTER 1

Abbott, W. C. *The Expansion of Europe.* New York: Henry Holt, 1918. Presents the European background to American history.

The American Heritage Book of Indians. New York: 1961. A thorough history of the Indians of the Americas from before the white man to the present, with many illustrations.

Cheyney, Edward P. *European Background of American History.* New York: Harper & Bros., 1904. An old book, but still basic.

Driver, Harold E. *Indians of North America.* Chicago: University of Chicago Press, 1961. The cultural history of the Indians of the Americas.

Morison, Samuel Eliot. *Admiral of the Ocean Sea.* 2 volumes. Boston: Little, Brown, 1942. The authoritative history of Columbus and his discoveries. (A one-volume edition is published as a Mentor paperback by The New American Library of World Literature under the title *Christopher Columbus, Mariner.*)

McNickle, D'Arcy. *They Came Here First.* Philadelphia: J. B. Lippincott, 1949. A history of the Indians before the white man.

CHAPTER 2

Bolton, Herbert E. *Spanish Borderlands.* New Haven: Yale University Press, 1921. Discusses Spanish exploration, settlement, government, and general colonial practices.

Brebner, John Bartlett. *The Explorers of North America, 1492–1806.* London, 1933. A good history of exploration in North America before 1806.

Carmer, Carl. *The Hudson.* New York: Farrar and Rinehart, 1939. A history of the Hudson River and the surrounding area.

Irving, Washington. *Knickerbocker's History of New York,* ed. Anne Carroll Moore. New York: Doubleday, Doran, 1928. A fictional and satirical account of life in Dutch New York.

Madariaga, Salvador de. *The Rise of the Spanish American Empire* and *The Fall of the Spanish American Empire.* London: Hollis & Carter, 1947. Two excellent books on Spain in America.

Parkman, Francis. *The Parkman Reader,* ed. Samuel Eliot Morison, Boston: Little, Brown, 1955. A condensation of a classic study of French colonization in America, and an excellent introduction to a well-known historian. Originally written in the late 19th century.

Wertenbaker, Thomas J. *Founding of American Civilization: The Middle Colonies.* New York: Charles Scribner's Sons, 1938. Included for the history of the Dutch and the Swedes in America.

Wrong, George M. *The Rise and Fall of New France.* 2 volumes. Toronto: Macmillan, 1928. A more modern study than Parkman's of the French in America.

CHAPTER 3

Beer, G. L. *The Origins of the British Colonial System, 1578–1660.* New York: Macmillan, 1908. An old book but one that presents the underlying reasons for British migration.

Hansen, Marcus Lee. *The Atlantic Migration, 1607–1860.* Cambridge: Harvard University Press, 1940. A history of foreign migration to America.

Notestein, Wallace. *The English People on the Eve of Colonization, 1603–1630.* New York: Harper & Bros., 1954. A view of the colonizers as they began to launch their ventures.

Wright, Louis. *The Atlantic Frontier: Colonial American Civilization, 1607–1763.* New York: Alfred A. Knopf, 1947. A good colonial history.

FOR GENERAL HISTORICAL INFORMATION:

Chitwood, Oliver P. *A History of Colonial America.* New York: Harper & Bros., 1931.

Nettels, Curtis P. *The Roots of American Civilization.* New York: F. S. Crofts, 1938.

Savelle, Max. *The Foundations of American Civilization.* New York: Henry Holt, 1942.

THE AMERICAN HERITAGE NEW ILLUSTRATED HISTORY OF THE UNITED STATES

PUBLISHED BY DELL PUBLISHING CO., INC.

George T. Delacorte, Jr., *Publisher* Helen Meyer, *President*
William F. Callahan, Jr., *Executive Vice-President*

Walter B. J. Mitchell, Jr., *Project Director;* Ross Claiborne, *Editorial Consultant;* William O'Gorman, *Editorial Assistant;* John Van Zwienen, *Art Consultant;* Rosalie Barrow, *Production Manager*

CREATED AND DESIGNED BY THE EDITORS OF AMERICAN HERITAGE MAGAZINE

James Parton, *Publisher;* Joseph J. Thorndike, Jr., *Editorial Director;* Bruce Catton, *Senior Editor;*
Oliver Jensen, *Editor;* Richard M. Ketchum, *Editor, Book Division;* Irwin Glusker, *Art Director*

ROBERT R. ENDICOTT, *Project Editor-in-Chief*

James Kraft, *Assistant Editor;* Nina Page, Evelyn H. Register, Lynn Marett, *Editorial Assistants;*
Lina Mainiero, *Copy Editor;* Murray Belsky, *Art Director;* Eleanor A. Dye, *Designer;* John Conley, *Assistant.*

CIVITAS. S Dominici sita in Hispaniola Indica Angliæ mag: nitudine fere æquales, ipsa urbs elegan: ter ab Hispanis extructa, et omnium circumiacentium insulis aura dat